D1123538

OROZCO IN GRINGOLAND

OROZCO

IN GRINGOLAND

The Years in New York

Alejandro Anreus

UNIVERSITY OF NEW MEXICO PRESS

ALBUQUERQUE

Orozco in Gringoland
The Years in New York
Alejandro Anreus

University of New Mexico Press
Albuquerque

*All images by José Clemente Orozco courtesy of the Instituto Nacional
de Bellas Artes y Literatura and the Estate of José Clemente Orozco
unless otherwise noted.*

Library of Congress Cataloging-in-Publication Data

Anreus, Alejandro.
    Orozco in gringoland : the years in New York / Alejandro Anreus.—1st ed.
        p. cm.
Includes bibliographical references (p.   ) and index.
        ISBN 0-8263-2067-8 (cloth) : alk. paper)
    1. Orozco, José Clemente, 1883–1949—Criticism and interpretation.
I. Title.
    ND259.07 A9 2001
    759.972—dc21

                                                                00-00945

Book design: Mina Yamashita

Para mi mujer,
Debra Blehart

Para mis hijos,
David Lawrence Rentkiewicz
e Isabel Maria Anreus

CONTENTS

All images are courtesy of the Instituto Nacional de Bellas Artes y Literatura and the Estate of José Clemente Orozco unless otherwise noted.

ACKNOWLEDGMENTS

This work began when, as a twelve-year-old boy, I encountered José Clemente Orozco's work through the books of both Alma Reed and MacKinley Helm at the Elizabeth Public Library in Elizabeth, New Jersey. I had become interested in art at age eleven and was reading everything I could find at the public library, coming home with books mostly on Italian and French artists. My grandmother, ever the Latin Americanist, suggested that I look for books on Cuban art (the country of my birth) or on other Latin American artists. She mentioned "Los Tres Grandes": Diego Rivera, David Alfaro Siqueiros (who was still alive in 1972), and Orozco. My grandmother recommended that I look at Orozco. Orozco's work moved me at twelve years of age, and it has continued to move me through the completion of first a doctoral dissertation and now this book twenty-nine years later.

When I did undergraduate work in art history at Kean College (now University) of New Jersey, I was fortunate to study under Alan Wallach, currently Ralph H. Wark Professor of Art and Art History, College of William and Mary. He opened the doors of art history to me, a young Cuban exile and the son of a factory worker. He made the discipline exciting and contextual, a method for reading reality and interpreting history. I will always be grateful for his encouragement, guidance, and friendship. My teachers at the Graduate and University Center, City University of New York, and scholars, colleagues, artists, dealers, collectors, the Orozco family, and others all over the United States and Mexico have helped me to understand the matrix of ideas emanating from the subject I have tackled. Among these, special thanks are due to Marlene Park, my dissertation advisor; Paul Avrich, leading historian of radicalism who clarified historical and political issues of Orozco's time; and Diana L. Linden, who talked with me about Orozco, muralists, and social realism and was supportive during the transformation of the dissertation into this book.

In Mexico, Doña Raquel Tibol, dean of Mexican art critics, answered many questions and pointed me in the right direction. The staffs at the Carrillo

Gil Museum and the Justino Fernández Library at the Universidad Nacional Autónoma de México (U.N.A.M.) as well as the archivists at the Casa Museo José Clemente Orozco and the Instituto Nacional de Bellas Artes y Literatura, were always willing to bring out works of art, books, magazines, papers, and photographic records. My friends Juan Mathé and his late wife, Marta, opened their home to me and drove me everywhere. Vicente and Estela Leñero were also supportive as always.

Many scholars have been helpful, most of all David Craven, who read my manuscript, made suggestions, and was supportive throughout the rewriting of this book. His own book on Diego Rivera is a model of critical scholarship. I am also grateful to Shifra M. Goldman for her comments and suggestions. At The Museum of Modern Art, I want to thank both Robert Storr and Judith Cousins of the Department of Painting and Sculpture. My "amigos de toda la vida," Miguel Socarrás, Manuel Pérez, Roberto Estopiñán, and Marion Grezsiak, were encouraging and supportive as always. Of these, Miguel was always

there to help me out of my computer nightmares. Special thanks to documentary filmmaker Ray Blanco, whose film on Orozco is an important contribution, for all his help and support.

I thank my family, including my mother, Margarita, and my aunt Gladys, for their love and support. My children, David and Isabel, were always patient and supportive of their "papi" whenever I had to work on Orozco. They share the dedication of this book with their mother. Most of all, I am grateful to my wife and friend, Debra Blehart. Deb never failed to listen, love, and challenge me; she always reminded me that we had a life beyond "el querido manco Orozco." I grew up hearing my grandmother tell me an old Catalan saying that one became a man only after planting a tree, having a child, and writing a book—with Deb, and thanks to her, I have done all three.

Finally, I am grateful to my editor at the University of New Mexico Press, Dana Asbury, for all of her work on this manuscript. ■

INTRODUCTION

"Los Tres Grandes" of the Mexican mural movement re-created a monumental, narrative painting that had a profound impact on the art of the Western hemisphere up to World War II. José Clemente Orozco (1883–1949) is both the oldest and least studied of the "Big Three" of the Mexican mural movement. From 1927 until 1934, Orozco lived in self-imposed exile in the United States and was based in New York City. In New York, Orozco, who did not visit Europe until 1932, first encountered a modernity radically different from his native Mexico's, whether expressed in art, design, economics, technology, or urbanism. The modernity of Mexico City was one thoroughly grounded in its many pasts: pre-Columbian, colonial, nineteenth-century positivism, the "modernismo" of symbolism and Rubén Darío, among others. The modernity of New York City seemed to have no past, was grounded in Protestant practicality, and was thoroughly industrial. For Orozco, modernity could mean an elimination of nineteenth-century academic dogmas and a liberation from its prejudices, as well as a synthesis of the best art of the past with the concerns of the present. Of course, the modern for Orozco was also the uneasy encounter between humans and the machine.

His engagement with New York City enabled Orozco

1

to expand his artistic vision. While in New York City, he produced important easel works, took up lithography (executing nineteen lithographs between 1928 and 1930), and painted two major murals: *Revolution and the Brotherhood of Man* at the New School for Social Research (1930–31) and *Dive Bomber and Tank* (1940) at The Museum of Modern Art, a portable mural executed during a brief return to the city. The New York years fit into his total output and career not just as an experimental period for the formal and thematic concerns that would be expressed in the more mature murals of Guadalajara (1936–39), but also as a time when Orozco produced some important easel work.

The New School mural has been studied from a formal and chronological perspective, yet its iconographic project and contextual locus remain unexplored. The portable mural for The Museum of Modern Art was only dealt with briefly by Alfred H. Barr Jr. in 1946. To respond to this hiatus, I will explore both of these murals in an integral and dynamic manner in order to examine context, form, and content.

The artist's greatest champion in the city was the occasional journalist Alma Reed (1889–1961). In fact, Reed opened the Delphic Studios gallery in October 1929 to promote Orozco's work, and in 1932 she wrote the first monograph on the artist. Nevertheless, Orozco had an uneasy relationship with his dealer, due in part to the economic and emotional demands placed upon the artist by the family he had left back in Mexico and the fact that he seems to have been romantically involved with Reed.

Orozco's stay in New York enabled him to develop a critical position toward the work of his compatriots (Diego Rivera in particular), especially with regard to their depiction of Mexican life and the revolution from what he would regard as a positive, even utopic, point of view. In contrast to this often celebratory view, Orozco proposed an essentially bleak and tragic view that is best expressed in the prints and paintings of the 1920s and early 1930s. While Rivera critically praised the assembly lines in Detroit, Orozco conversely stressed the brutality of modernization and urban life. Siqueiros and Rivera were Marxists who were fascinated with the technology brought about by American capitalism and the potential that they believed it harbored for the future. Orozco's political background was also dissident, but it was based in anarcho-syndicalism. He came to understand that United States modernity, as expressed in New York City, was a sophisticated product of capitalist ideology and Western modernization, with very destructive intrinsic forces. Like many anarchists worldwide after the triumph of the 1917 Bolshevik Revolution and its repressive aftermath, Orozco became skeptical of whether revolutions in general could bring out the positive promise of capitalism. This skepticism, if not despair, is visible in many of his graphic and easel works of Mexican scenes, which often seem to offer no historical redemption whatsoever.

Sources

Despite the significance of Orozco and the growing demand for studies of Latin American art and especially murals, studies of Orozco are few and generally inadequate. Five books in English have dealt with Orozco's work. These are Reed's 1932 monograph, *José Clemente Orozco*; MacKinley Helm's 1953 biography, *Man of Fire*; Reed's *Orozco* of 1956; the Oxford University Museum of Modern Art's 1980 *Orozco!* catalog; and Laurance Hurlburt's 1989 *The Mexican Muralists in the United States*. The first, a collection of black-and-white images with a one-page introduction by the author, scarcely addresses the historic importance of his work. The second, a traditional chronological biography, demonstrates Helm's lack of familiarity with Mexican culture, as well as his rudimentary knowledge of the Spanish language. Although a primary source, the Reed biography must be read with considerable caution because of the author's unduly subjective viewpoint. The Oxford catalog presents an overview of Orozco's life and work that is too reliant on secondary and tertiary sources. Hurlburt's more recent book is foundational. It lays out the itineraries of Orozco, Rivera, and Siqueiros in the United States and presents previously unknown information regarding patronage. Solid and well researched, it is nonetheless limited from an interpretive vantage point. In addition, Hurlburt omits a sustained iconographic reading and an ideological critique of the murals; he treats Orozco's New School mural far too quickly and ignores altogether the portable Museum of Modern Art mural of 1940.

There are three main works on Orozco in Spanish, and they are mere generalized treatments of the artist and his works: *Orozco forma e idea* (Justino Fernández, 1942), *Orozco* (Luis Cardoza y Aragón, 1983), and *Orozco: Una vida para el arte* (Raquel Tibol, 1983). A fourth book, *Orozco: Una relectura* (Xavier Moyssén, ed., 1983), is an anthology of essays that vary in depth and critical content. While building upon and responding to the art historical literature of the past fifty years in both Spanish and English, my book is also meant to extend greatly the interpretive range with which Orozco's art has been examined.

In terms of methodology, my work is both critically detached and historically engaged, indebted to the various models offered by Shifra M. Goldman's *Contemporary Mexican Painting in a Time of Change* (1981), Juan Martínez's *Cuban Art and National Identity* (1994), and, most importantly, David Craven's *Diego Rivera as Epic Modernist* (1997). These works examine the complex relationships between aesthetics and politics through critical perspectives that are thoroughly grounded in the historical and cultural contexts of each theme.

This book begins with Orozco's reasons for leaving Mexico at the end of 1927—namely, the changing political environment under President Plutarco Elías Calles and its effects on cultural politics. My study concludes with Orozco's last visit to New York in 1945. The book is organized chronologically/thematically, so that the focus on artistic experimentation and production could be analyzed more readily with recourse to the historical context that spawned it. In addition to Orozco studies and general mural literature, I also examine the cultural history of New York City during the 1920s and 1930s, including the founding of The Museum of Modern Art and its sponsorship of Mexican art, along with the reception to and perception of the presences of Orozco, Rivera, and Siqueiros in New York City through the general press, as well as the interest and presentation of Mexican art by the commercial art galleries.

In order to explicate the artistic intention at issue in the murals and easel and graphic works, a critical reading of Orozco's correspondence while in New York City was essential. Some of it is published, such as the letters to Jean Charlot (1971) and the letters to Margarita Valladares de Orozco (1987); some of it remains unpublished. Deciphering the artist's slim and straightforward autobiography, *Autobiografía* (1945), was important in the reconstruction of how the years in New York City had an impact on his artistic practice and ideological viewpoint. One manuscript interview with Orozco is in the José Gómez Sicre Papers in Miami, Florida. It dates from 1946 and was conducted in New York City by the Cuban-born critic-curator José Gómez Sicre. It had not been cited in print until now. Among the other unpublished primary sources I have used is Orozco's correspondence to his wife that has not appeared in print, as well as various personal interviews and questionnaires of artists and critics who either knew Orozco or were familiar with the time period that I am dealing with in this study.

In sum, I examine Orozco's artistic production while he was in the City of New York: two murals and several easel paintings, drawings, and lithographs. I interpret these works through the cultural and socio-political context of the paintings and through the content depicted in their subjects. I also analyze these works qua visual languages endowed with distinctive formal power in their own right.

LEAViNG MEXiCo iN 1927

In 1927, when Mexico entered the second year of the Cristero War, President Plutarco Elías Calles crushed the anarcho-syndicalist labor movement.[1] These two seemingly unrelated events are linked in Orozco's background. Although anticlerical and against institutional Roman Catholicism, throughout Orozco's work there is evident a spiritual, if non-religious, sensibility that infuses his images with an ethical and virulent concern against corruption and injustice. At times he is a kindred spirit to moralist expressionist artists like Georges Rouault. Anarcho-syndicalism is not just the artist's only known political association; anarchism is often marked by an apocalyptic view of change, which is reflected in much of Orozco's work. Therefore, both the Cristero War and the elimination of the anarcho-syndicalist labor movement in 1927 are part and parcel of Orozco's cultural and political baggage.

On December 11, 1927, Orozco departed from Mexico on what was to be his second trip to the United States.[2] His previous trip lasted two years, from 1917 to 1919. These visits, as we shall see, were not unrelated. In his *Autobiografía*, Orozco dedicates chapters 6 and 7, a total of twelve pages, to his first sojourn in the United States.[3] In these pages we find the anecdote on the destruction (due to their allegedly immoral subject matter) of some sixty watercolors by United States Customs officers in Laredo, Texas. He then proceeds to describe his visit to San Francisco, his work there as a sign and movie-poster painter, and the general patriotic and anti-German atmosphere at the end of World War I, which as an anarchist Orozco repudiated as nationalistic and ethnocentric. Orozco also discusses his eventual decision to go to New York. During his first day in the city, Orozco encountered David Alfaro Siqueiros and his wife, Graciela Amador, who were on their way to Europe. They spent a number of days together seeing the sights of the "imperial city" (Orozco's caustic words), traveling by subway to Brooklyn, and arguing about the relationship between technology and art.[4] Orozco insists in the text that he took the opposite side of the argument simply to make it lively, even though he does not recall which side he took. Siqueiros remembers it differently:

> I could not hold back my old admiration for such a "powerful work of engineering." With the usual enthusiasm of always regarding this work, I told José Clemente Orozco: "One can barely imagine what it means to drill eighty miles of rock to make these trains run with such speed and precision, which is one of its great merits." Once again, José Clemente Orozco turned his face towards me with his furious owl eyes, screaming: "You are an idiot. This is nothing portentous. Anyone can make this!" Then to get him more upset, something which was my custom, I said to him with the utmost sarcasm, knowing that this way I would offend him: "This is worth a thousand times more than all the work of your famous Rodin" (which he liked a great deal). Then the train came, we jumped in it quickly, and already sitting, José Clemente Orozco came back on the attack: "Idiotic provincial. Idiotic provincial."[5]

Already in this brief argument we see Orozco's dystopic, even apocalyptic stand toward technology. Again, this view is consistent with certain strains of anarchism.

FIG. 1: *Dios Padre,* 1923–26, fresco.

After Siqueiros's departure, Orozco went on to explore Harlem, Coney Island (where, quite revealingly, the side-shows with their freaks caught his fancy and preference for the grotesque), tattoo parlors, and the Flea Circus. He ends this chapter with a sarcastic meditation on the premural art milieu in Mexico, where anyone (given colors, canvases, and brushes) could be an art student. This is obviously an attack on painter-educator Alfredo Ramos Martínez and his visionary open-air art school in Santa Anita.[6]

Undoubtedly, the most interesting aspect in the first New York section of the *Autobiografía* is the artist's mention of Harlem and Coney Island, both marginal and exotic places that he would frequent after 1927 and from which he would derive one easel painting and one lithograph. Perhaps Orozco's attraction to places such as these connects with Charles Baudelaire's sense of modernity as interwoven with marginality.

Orozco then returned to Mexico, married Margarita Valladares, and executed murals at the Escuela Nacional Preparatoria San Ildefonzo (1923–26), Casa de los Azulejos (1925), and Escuela Industrial de Orizaba (1926). The

FIG. 2: *Franciscano,*
1923–26, fresco.

Preparatoria murals are his first monumental works, filled
with experiments, indecisions, and transitions. On the first
floor we see his debt to Botticelli in the *Maternity* panel.
His experience as a political cartoonist is reflected in the
caricature-like panel *The Rich Dine While the Workers Quar-
rel*, as well as on the second floor in such works as *The Law
and Justice* and *Dios Padre* (fig. 1). This last panel in particular shows Orozco's vitriolic draftsmanship at the service of his dissident sensibility; God is a bloated old man
in anachronistic white robes surrounded by devils who
torment the poor and by the haughty rich who will most
definitely be saved. The more stylistically focused Orozco
is found in the panels whose subjects are either the conquest
(*Franciscano* panels [fig. 2], *Cortés and Malinche*) or the revolution (*La Trinchera* [fig. 3], *The Farewell to the Mother*). In
these works Orozco achieves a purity of bold, monumental forms, with a depth of feeling as intense as a Greek
tragedy. These works also possess a sensibility similar to
certain aspects of German expressionism, yet where and
how could Orozco have been exposed to the German ex-
pressionists this early in his career? The arches in the cor-
ridor of the Preparatoria contain decorations comprising
powerful hands, hammers, and sickles—remember that at
this time Orozco was a member of the Sindicato de Obreros

FIG. 3: *La trinchera,*
1923–26, fresco.

Técnicos, Pintores y Escultores, founded in 1923, whose
tenets and symbols resembled those of the Mexican Communist Party. Opposed to the continuation of both traditional patronage and forms, easel painting in particular, the
Sindicato's ideological worldview was socialist with both
agrarian and urban dimensions.

In 1925, while work at the Preparatoria was interrupted,
Orozco painted in the private residence Casa de los Azulejos
the mural *Omniciencia* (fig. 4). This work was commissioned
by the owner, Francisco Sergio Iturbe. The subject is an allegory of theosophic content—a form of philosophical thought
characterized by the belief in a transcendent reality that can
be perceived or experienced mystically. In this mural nude
figures of both genders represent a creation story.[7] The work
of William Blake (much admired among theistic anarchists) could be a key influence here, particularly since
his spiritualism harbored a critique of capitalism and
modernization.

The last mural of this period, *Revolución social* (fig. 5) at the Escuela Industrial de Orizaba, again takes up the theme of the revolution. On a wall the shape of an inverted U, Orozco depicted workers and soldiers doing masonry work in the top panel and weeping women (in one panel hiding a scared soldier of the old regime) in the lower two. The angles of the figures in movement give this simple work a great deal of grace. The content—the revolution building the future—is so life-affirming as to bring Rivera's work to mind. At this time Orozco was also involved in the execution of a number of easel pictures, such as *La casa blanca* and *El muerto*, which would be completed by 1928 in the United States.[8]

On January 28, 1924, José Vasconcelos, the secretary of public education and one of the key figures responsible for the execution of murals in public buildings, offered his resignation to President Alvaro Obregón. It was formally accepted on July 3.[9] A number of ideological and aesthetic convergencies link Orozco and Vasconcelos. The late poet and essayist Octavio Paz has stated this clearly:

> Orozco moves us, moreover, by another admirable quality: he is a free spirit. A true rebel. Because of his ideas as well as because of his temperament Orozco bears more than one similarity to Vasconcelos. They both began as revolutionaries and both ended up as admirers of Cortés, the bogeyman of liberals and revolutionaries. The Mexican Reaction (written as it should be, with a capital R) has in Vasconcelos and in Orozco its two loftiest and most authentic expressions in this century. Both were deeply religious, although Orozco never fell into Vasconcelos' bigotry or his political aberrations. On the contrary, Orozco was one of the first to see the similarities between Hitlerism and Stalinism. He was a passionate spirit and yet strangely perceptive and clearsighted. A really free man and artist who—something almost unheard of in Mexico—had no fear of using his freedom, no matter what the consequences.[10]

FIG. 4: *Omniciencia*, 1925, fresco.

FIG. 5: *Revolución social*, 1926, fresco.

What is interesting in the Vasconcelos-Orozco conver-
gence is that both men felt a deep connection with Western civilization, from the Greek and Roman worlds to the
Judeo-Christian tradition, and neither was understanding of
the greatness of the pre-Columbian cultures. Vasconcelos's
disillusionment with the Mexican Revolution led him to a
right-wing, Hispano-centric position. Not so with Orozco,
who never embraced Catholicism the way Vasconcelos did
and who in his mural and easel paintings was critical of
both the pre-Columbian world and the Spanish Conquest.

In August, after Vasconcelos's resignation, all of the
artists painting in the Preparatoria were dismissed, and
José Manuel Puig Casauranc was appointed the new secretary of public education. Rivera weathered this crisis and
established a good relationship with the new secretary.
Rivera's ability to continue painting murals throughout
this period reflects a complex situation; in the words of
David Craven, "he knew that the meaning of his art was

situated at the unsettled intersection of broadly contested interests both within a contradictory, nonmonolithic state and between this federal government and various popular movements periodically mobilized to influence its direction, sometimes with undeniable success."[11]

Orozco eventually returned to the Preparatoria in 1926 and completed his work there. He also restored the work that had been defaced by students in 1924.

At this point the initial enthusiastic phase of the mural movement in Mexico was over. Some of the artists went to the provinces to execute murals; others took up easel painting.[12] Rivera continued to receive governmental patronage; under the Calles administration, he completed murals at Chapingo (1926–27) and the Secretaría de Educación Pública—his masterpiece (finished in 1928). These murals contain some of his most cohesive and powerful ideological narratives. They were problematic to some of his patrons, yet the nonmonolithic identity of the Mexican state at this time allowed his radical message to get through. In 1930, Rivera painted murals in the Palacio de Cortés in Cuernavaca; the patron was Dwight W. Morrow, the United States ambassador who had become a friend of President Calles and who was a lawyer for the J. P. Morgan Trust. Morrow, on behalf of the trust, pressured Calles to stop the nationalization of oil fields. Calles, during his time in power (as president from 1924 to 1928 and as a behind-the-scenes caudillo from 1929 to 1934), abandoned the Mexican Revolution's agenda of agrarian reform and workers' rights in favor of the interests of foreign investors. This change was partly due to very direct pressure from the United States government, as well as Calles's personal greed and corruption. On the cultural front, Calles further dismantled the cultural programs of Vasconcelos, mural painting included.

By mid-1927, Orozco found Mexico without possibilities for his art, yet his reason for departing must also be seen within the contemporary sociopolitical background, not simply as an aesthetic decision.[13] Orozco's only known political association was with the anarchism of the anarcho-syndicalist Casa del Obrero Mundial. The casa's basic political positions were the usual ones associated with anarcho-syndicalism; they were an urban and secular organization, opposed to the agrarian and religious forces of both Zapata and Villa, and they favored the emancipation of the working class through revolutionary means. In periods of transition their position was to empower the working class through an independent labor movement, which would use the strike as a means to gain workers' rights and weaken the capitalist system. As anarchists, those in the casa were suspicious of the power of the state, even though during this period they allied themselves with the most centralizing forces within the struggle, the Constitutionalists, much to the disapproval of older anarchists such as Ricardo Flores Magón. This association came through the painter Gerardo Murillo (1875–1964), known as Dr. Atl. When the casa took the Constitutionalists' (Generals Carranza and Obregón) side during the struggle against the forces of Villa and Zapata in 1915, Dr. Atl enlisted Orozco to join. Orozco became the political cartoonist of the casa's newspaper, *La Vanguardia*.[14] Two of his covers (fig. 6) depict harlot-like females in aggressive positions. These women have dark lips and eyes and have much in common with Orozco's prostitutes from *The House of Tears* series, as well as with symbolist femme fatales, the kind the artist might have encountered in European as well as Mexican magazine illustrations of the period. On one cover the woman's face takes up most of the page; the face is behind a hatchet and a knife. She is all smiles. Under her face is the line: "I am the Revolution, The Destroyer." On the other cover she is transformed into a Judith with black stockings, bloody knife in one hand, decapitated head in the other. These simple drawings allow us to see Orozco's dark humor; the revolution, like a harlot, is attractive, but something dark and violent will follow—venereal disease with the harlot, death and destruction with the revolution.

After the successes of 1915, the casa opened headquarters in different Mexican cities and became a force within the labor movement. By 1916, Obregón ordered them to disband as a revolutionary movement. They then evolved into the Confederación General de Trabajadores (CGT) in

FIG. 6: Covers of *La Vanguardia*, 1916.

1921. In 1927, the CGT supported the strikes of the militant petroleum workers in Tampico and the railroad workers nationwide. These workers were not only fighting for better working conditions and rights but also for the unfulfilled promises of the revolution, which included the nationalization of the petroleum fields and control over foreign-owned industries. On February 9, 1927, the CGT called for a general strike throughout the Federal District (Mexico, D.F.). President Calles dispatched troops to protect company property. When workers were shot by government troops, the strikers retaliated with sabotage.[15] The government kept up the pressure. Early on, Calles had supported the labor leader Luis Morones and his less radical Confederación Regional Obrera Mexicana (CROM). Eventually Morones became corrupt, and CROM did the government's, not the workers', bidding. Orozco actually caricatured Morones for the libertarian rag sheet *L'ABC* (fig. 7), where he depicts the labor leader in bloomers and a bra, fat and hairy and wearing a ring and earring, a switchblade stuck in his garter. On the bloomer are written the words "Presidential Ambition." Morones, as drawn by Orozco, is the government's fat and grotesque but reliable whore.

The year 1927 was a watershed for the anarcho-syndicalist labor movement (as represented by the CGT), because it was to be disempowered by the government. Although it continued to exist until its official demise in July 1931, after 1927 it was ineffective.[16] Orozco, as someone who had been involved with the anarcho-syndicalist movement as a political cartoonist and possibly a rank-and-file member, had to be affected by the persecution and eventual repression of his one-time comrades.

The other sociopolitical event of this time was the Cristero War (1926–29).[17] It began as a conflict between the Mexican hierarchy, the papal nuncio, and the Obregón government (although it escalated under Calles) over the Church's criticism of anti-Catholic articles in the constitution and government policies. As a protest the Church went on strike, suspending masses and other sacraments across the country. The Liga Defensora de la Libertad Religiosa was formed, and by 1926, when the battles started, it had created a committee of war. The majority of cristero soldiers were peasants who had been followers of either Zapata or Villa. They wanted to continue to worship freely, and they also wanted the land that had been promised to them in the 1910s. If the government was brutal in its persecution of the cristeros, the cristeros themselves committed many atrocities, such as the torture and execution of rural teachers working with the peasantry in the countryside. The cristeros opposed literacy, since they saw it as an enemy of religion that could only help the secular Mexican government. Numbering some twenty thousand in 1927, the cristeros took over Jalisco, Colima, and Nayarit.[18] In 1929, at the behest of Ambassador Morrow (who, although a patron of Rivera, had criticized the strong anticlericalism of his murals), the Mexican government and the Roman Catholic Church signed an agreement of mutual recognition. The clergy would not be allowed to wear religious habits in public, vote, or own private property. The lay leaders of the cristero troops

Foto: cortesía del Museo Nacional de Arte.

13. Caricatura publicada en la revista *L'ABC*, 9 de agosto de 1925, colección Hemeroteca Nacional.

FIG. 7: Caricature of Luis Morones from *L'ABC*. Hemeroteca Nacional.

went into exile. The troops themselves were abandoned by the church hierarchy, and they either surrendered, were imprisoned, or were executed by the government.[19]

Orozco, who was born in Jalisco and had family there, had to be concerned about this religious civil war. Although he was profoundly anticlerical, his moralistic vision was based on a Christian ethic. Therefore, there is a connection between Orozco and the cristero peasants. The connection lies in Orozco reflecting the reality of the cristero peasant in his depictions of Christ. Betrayed and abandoned, they had much in common with the images of Christ painted by Orozco from the Preparatoria murals to the easel works of the 1940s—working-class, marginal figures involved in a struggle that is to be lost.

Years later, Orozco would recall to his friend and collector Dr. Antonio Luna Arroyo that in 1927 Mexico was a *pinche pais* in every way—in art, politics, even daily life.[20] He had to leave. In time he would be followed by both Rivera and Siqueiros to the United States, who were also in search of mural commissions.

To facilitate his departure, Orozco sold two oil paintings, *Combate* to Foreign Secretary Genaro Estrada, which gave him enough funds for train fare and three months' subsistence, and *Soldaderas* to the secretary of public education, José Manuel Puig Casauranc. He probably left the funds from this last sale with his wife, two small sons, and one-month-old daughter, who stayed behind in Mexico.[21]

Orozco left Mexico City by train on December 11, 1927.[22] He was headed for New York. His reasons for leaving had a lot to do with the need for new opportunities for his art, but he was also distancing himself from a country where his former anarcho-syndicalist comrades were being repressed and cristero peasants were at war with the government. He was leaving behind a *pinche pais*.

GRINGOLAND: NEW YORK CITY, ALMA REED, AND THE DELPHIC STUDIOS

When José Clemente Orozco arrived in New York City shortly before Christmas 1927, he wrote his wife:

> My adored little wife: Here I am finally in Gringoland, trying to make a name for myself and promote my work. This incredible city, part amusement park and part growing monstrosity, has changed a great deal since I was last here. It is very cold and windy. For now I don't see any possibility for anything, not until after the holidays. . . . Everybody is partying now. Send me Anita's [Brenner] address. For now I am living at 316 W. 23rd St. Give many kisses to my little parrots and you receive the heart of your sad
>
> Clemente.[1]

The city had indeed changed since he was last there almost a decade before. In the 1920s, a number of elements had come together in New York City: natural resources that were unlimited, a population that was multiracial and multilingual, and opportunities for a more pluralistic and democratic society.[2]

After World War I, the United States, and particularly New York City, entered the modern era. The 1920s was the decade of jazz, skyscrapers (although some of these were not completed until the 1930s), new technologies, gangsters, Prohibition, the Harlem Renaissance, and the prose styles of Willa Cather, F. Scott Fitzgerald, Zora Neale Hurston, and Ernest Hemingway. All of this dynamism would come to an end with the stock market crash in October 1929. In the meantime, "modern America, led by New York, was free to promote, not an egalitarian society, but something like an egalitarian popular and mass culture, aggressively appropriating forms and ideas across race, class, and gender lines."[3] Still, from the Roaring Twenties through the Great Depression, there was another United States: one where lynchings took place in the South, where immigrant labor was exploited, and where radicals like Sacco and Vanzetti were executed. But Orozco was coming from a country torn by social conflict (the struggles of the Mexican Revolution exhausted the country with seven years of fighting and 2 million dead) and religious strife and a society still burdened with the legacies and customs of the nineteenth and previous centuries. New York City in 1927 was radically modern and far less disrupted.

The October 1927 exhibition calendar in *Art News* listed fifty-nine galleries, most of which exhibited antique furniture, Old Masters, and Orientalia. Only a dozen or so, such as the Kraushaar, Macbeth, Daniel, and the Intimate galleries, displayed American art. Nonetheless, the Sterner, Weyhe, and Downtown galleries had exhibited or were to exhibit Mexican art. Paintings by Diego Rivera were exhibited in New York City as early as 1916, and Rufino Tamayo had exhibited his paintings at the Weyhe Gallery in the fall of 1926.[4] Starting in the mid-1920s and lasting through the early 1930s, New York (and other large cities such as Los Angeles and Philadelphia) would get its share of the "Mexican art invasion." Orozco would partake of this phenomenon, but always with reservations.[5]

Again, unlike Rivera and Siqueiros, who had experienced

and contributed to modernism in Paris firsthand, New York was Orozco's first encounter with a secular society in love with itself and its technologies. Rivera lived in Paris roughly from 1909 to 1921; Siqueiros lived there in 1919–20. Although born in the nineteenth century, both of them possessed the open, experimental sensibility associated with the twentieth century. Not so with Orozco, who was essentially a man of the mainstream nineteenth century or, at the very least, one caught in the crosscurrents between the two centuries. Orozco's moralistic outlook is definitely premodern if not Victorian, as is his cautious, nearly methodical approach to formal experimentation in his art. This is evident in the ambiguous love-hate relationship in which he deals with what he termed as "part amusement park and part growing monstrosity" that was New York City.

Orozco's reactions and opinions during his stay in New York City are best found in his correspondence with fellow artist Jean Charlot (1898–1979) and Orozco's wife, Margarita Valladares (1898–1993). Orozco exchanged letters with Charlot from December 1927 through February 1929. He wrote to his wife throughout his stay of 1927–34 and during later visits in 1940 and 1945, and she did visit her husband in both New York and Hanover, New Hampshire, during his different stays. Most of 1928 was a period of solitude in which Orozco made few contacts with the New York art world; therefore, communication with Charlot at this time was vital to Orozco. The correspondence with Charlot stopped, due to misunderstandings and a sense of competition between the two artists, roughly at the same time that Orozco joined the circle of friends around Eva Sikelianos and Alma Reed.

What did Orozco see in New York? Whom did he meet? Based on Orozco's letters to Charlot, we know that he visited New York's galleries with regularity (even if he failed to mention which galleries). Before the end of December 1927, Orozco visited exhibitions of Picasso and Renoir:

> Yesterday I saw two exhibitions, Picasso and Renoir.
> Of the first drawings: figures copied, it seems, from
> greek vases in museums. No more than two or three

lines. Very repetitive. Pen and ink drawings. A very able hand. Drawings in pencil with "much volume." I made desperate efforts to become enthusiastic, but did not achieve it. You and I have drawings one hundred times better. A landscape in pastel, which according to W[alter]. Pach is exactly the same as Derain. Renoir made quite an impression on me, I liked him extraordinarily. I lost an hour and a half seeing five or six small pictures. The rest is not that good, they must be studies or youthful works. In the evening I visited W[alter] Pach.[6]

It is interesting to read in Orozco's own words his admiration for Renoir, who was his antithesis, a painter of joy and sensuality. Yet it demonstrates from the start his deep curiosity and his receptiveness to new visual experiences, particularly in New York where, at the age of forty-four, he was encountering a version of the "modern" radically different from the one he had encountered in Mexico.

Among the first persons whom Orozco visited in New York City was the art critic and painter Walter Pach (1883–1958). Orozco had met Pach when the critic had visited Mexico in 1922 to lecture at the Summer School for Foreigners at the National University. In the same letter to Charlot, Orozco writes of Pach's cordiality, his magnificent studio, his great admiration for Picasso, and his own awful paintings and good pictures hanging on the walls: a head by Derain and prints by Cézanne and Signorelli.[7] The acquaintance did not develop into something more. Orozco believed that Pach did not consider him a serious artist; Pach did not appreciate Orozco's opinion regarding his own mediocre talents as a painter.

Orozco's visits to galleries and museums continued. In January 1928 he visited exhibitions at New York University and the Valentiner gallery. At these, he was quite taken by Matisse, even while recognizing the dramatic differences between himself and Matisse:

But one of the Matisse's was something very new for me: extraordinary color and so fine, fine that it becomes like china paper and the silk of the colors, yet

it never loses its plasticity. The exhibition at the
Valentiner gallery of which I send you a checklist, is
immensely better, equally Matisse and Derain; this
is the first time that I am seeing modern art, to the day,
without missing ancient art. Pure painting, without
doubts. Grace. Naturalness. Joy. It gives great pleasure
to see these pictures and one remains content and
satisfied for the rest of the day. The Derain's are
busts of women, fleshy and profound. Matisse is
color and light, freshness and serenity. These painters are among those who live in the garden and
have girlfriends with the five o'clock tea, salons,
the good society, good drink and good bed. We are
the revolutionaries, the damned and starving.[8]

In New York Orozco saw eighteenth-century art, dis-
liking Sorolla's paintings at the Hispanic Society while
admiring works by El Greco, Goya, and Velázquez. He found
Picasso's pictures disconcerting yet unforgettable. American
painters he considered a tragic failure; to him the true American artists were those who made the machines.[9]

The one acquaintance from Mexico who was in New York
at this time and willing to help Orozco with her contacts was
Anita Brenner (1905–1974). Brenner was a Mexican-born
journalist of American Jewish parents. She had studied in
Texas, and in Mexico she was something of a cicerone for
visiting Americans during the early 1920s. Although in time
Orozco would see her as an advocate of Rivera's work over
his, Brenner was the first person to take Orozco to parties
and introduce him to potential patrons. When Brenner came
to New York in the summer of 1927, she brought with her
some of Orozco's drawings from the series *México en
revolución*.[10] She also published an essay on Orozco in the
October 1927 issue of *The Arts*. Entitled "A Mexican Rebel,"
the article begins with a brief statement about the destruc-
tiveness of the Mexican Revolution; it then places Orozco as
its rebellious witness, for whom this historical process has
been a *via crucis*. Brenner goes on to discuss Orozco's *La casa
del llanto* series, the murals at the Preparatoria, and some
drawings. She concludes with the sentences, "Destroying and

creating, he suffers. He has a habit of pain."[11] Brenner would also introduce Orozco to Alma Reed (1889–1961), his future patron, dealer, and biographer (fig. 8).

In June 1928, Orozco would write Margarita:

> Anita told me the other day that there are possibilities of my selling a drawing and small picture of the ones I have made here. A Miss Alma Reed who was the fiancee of Carrillo Puerto, that governor of Yucatán who was killed, is interested in the drawing; she liked my works a lot, but naturally I was not introduced to her.[12]

Alma Reed

In a letter of August 2, 1928, Orozco mentions Alma Reed for the second time:

> To tell you that I have just received a letter from Alma Reed, whom I have not met, but she is a friend of Tablada and the person that Anita showed my drawings to in days past. She tells me that for a while she has been a profound admirer of mine, and that "The entire series on the Mexican revolution holds a very intimate appeal to me, but one of them, Cemetery scene, is irresistible" and she includes 20 dol. towards the 100, the price of the drawing. She wants to come to my studio and bring a friend to talk about the publication of I don't know what. My luck is changing a little bit, Miti. God listens to you![13]

Who was Alma Reed? Born Alma Marie Sullivan in San Francisco on June 17, 1889, she was the great-granddaughter of Irish immigrants. Her mother, Adelaide Murphy, a housewife, gave birth to ten children, Alma being the oldest. Her father, Eugene Sullivan, was an unsuccessful entrepreneur who doted on his eldest daughter. Alma did not attend college, but by the time she was twenty-four she was writing a human interest column for *The Call*, a socialist publication, under the pen name of Mrs. Goodfellow.[14]

In 1921, through this very column, Reed (in 1915, she married Samuel Reed, whom she would later divorce) saved the life of Simon Ruíz. A young Mexican on death

FIG. 8: Alma Reed
in New York City, c. 1928.

row in California, Ruíz was convicted of a crime he did
not commit. Part of the problem with the case was that
the accused did not speak English and could not be understood. This situation was compounded by racism and
xenophobia against Mexicans. In her column, Reed re-
viewed the case and its inconsistencies and essentially
moved public opinion in favor of Ruíz. When the governor of California pardoned Ruíz, Mexicans in California
saw Reed as a heroine, and thus President Obregón invited
her to visit Mexico as his guest. Reed visited Mexico in 1923,
this time reporting on the archaeological excavations in
Yucatán for the *New York Times*.[15] In Mérida, the capital of
Yucatán, Reed met and fell in love with the socialist governor Felipe Carrillo Puerto. They were to be married in
1924, after he had secured a divorce. Reed went back to
San Francisco to arrange the wedding plans. While she
was away, right-wing forces assassinated Carrillo Puerto
during the abortive rebellion led by Adolfo de la Huerta

during 1924–25. De la Huerta refused to recognize the government of General Alvaro Obregón as legitimate. Together with General Guadalupe Suárez, he took up arms against the Obregón regime. This rebellion galvanized the political views of the Mexican muralists, as evident in the manifesto published in *El Machete* in 1924.

By the time Orozco met Reed in the summer of 1928, she had traveled throughout Europe, lived in Greece for two years where she translated the poetry of Angelos Sikelianos, and was living on Fifth Avenue with Eva Sikelianos, the poet's widow.[16] Before he met Reed, Orozco had only one opportunity to exhibit his work in New York City. This was a group exhibition of Mexican art held at the Art Center at 65 East Fifty-sixth Street from January 19 through February 14, 1928.[17] Organized by Frances Flynn Paine, editor of the magazine *Mexican Folkways*, and presented under the auspices of the Mexican government, it contained works by Rivera, Charlot, Maximo Pacheco, Antonio Ruíz, Roberto Montenegro, Orozco, and others. The selection of works favored picturesque or folksy themes, thereby presenting a distorted picture of Mexican art at that time. Along with the paintings, Mexican crafts were also for sale. Orozco found the exhibition to be a total failure, badly installed and essentially an excuse to push Mexican folk art: "the gallery is bad, pure amateurs and beginners, the space is dark, the director an imbecile, complete disorder, eight days [after the opening] and still no catalogue. . . . I must tell you that the only object of this exhibition is to sell 'popular mexican crafts,' which is a business, for which our paintings served as propaganda posters."[18]

Orozco's first mention of Reed to Charlot is in a letter of September 1928:

> Miss Alma Reed, a beautiful woman, indulges in mythologizing [he refers to the cult of Greek mythology and folk arts in the Sikelianos circle]. She admires me and purchased one of my tragic drawings.[19]

By mid-September, Orozco had met Eva Sikelianos (whose portrait he would be painting a month later) through Reed. Sikelianos bought a painting of Orozco's for $300, and he was invited to visit their ashram at 12 Fifth Avenue.[20] Orozco's nine months of solitude in New York were over.

Orozco recalled the ashram years later in his autobiography:

> The literary-revolutionary salon of Mrs. Sikelianos was well attended. Some days Greeks came, among them doctor Kalimacos, patriarch of the Greek church in New York. One heard modern Greek, spoken to perfection by the owners of the house. Other days bronze-colored hindus with turbans came, followers of the cause of Mahatma Gandhi. Majestically Mrs. Sarojini Naidu would enter dressed in the custom of her country, showing between her eyebrows the distinctive red mark of her elevated caste, and followed by a group of maidens and secretaries, dressed similarly with their dresses and veils of colors, stitched in gold.[21]

At the ashram, Orozco not only met Kalimacos and Naidu but also the Dutch poet Leonard Van Hopen and the Lebanese poet and graphic artist Kahlil Gibran.[22] In this environment, both literature and politics were constant topics of discussion, discussions where the artist was either an active participant or a careful listener. The subject of Prometheus and other Greek myths was familiar to Orozco before his contact with the ashram. In the intellectual milieu of Mexico City during the early 1920s, Greek myths and their literary expressions were discussed and popularized by both José Vasconcelos and Alfonso Reyes.[23] It was in the Reed-Sikelianos circle where Orozco encountered the subject again, a visual clue of which would be his Pomona College mural of 1930. Yet the dual international/nationalistic aspects of the Reed-Sikelianos circle, with its Greek, Indian, and Mexican components, is most clearly felt in Orozco's New School of Social Research mural of 1931, where the stress is on national liberation in a postcolonial world.

During the week of September 28, 1928, Reed and Sikelianos hosted a modest exhibition of Orozco's works in their apartment. Drawings from the *México en revolución* series, some unidentified easel pictures, and a self-portrait (later destroyed by Orozco) were displayed.[24] Reed wrote Orozco regarding the exhibition:

> The interest in your exhibit grows. Yesterday we had several very important people here, some of whom are returning today with the owners of galleries and with wealthy prospective purchasers. We feel that in view of this continued interest that it would be wiser to keep the exhibition here until Friday night. There is a likelihood too of some portrait orders, so we think that it would be well to have your marvelous portrait of yourself here. . . . There will be some heads of galleries here today including Marie Sterner. I think that I shall have some news for you tomorrow evening.[25]

Marie Sterner, wife of realist painter Albert Sterner, did indeed visit Orozco's exhibition at the Reed-Sikelianos apartment. She offered Orozco his first one-person exhibition in New York City in the coming month of October.

Mexico in Revolution opened at the Fifty-seventh Street Galleries of Marie Sterner on October 10, 1928, and ran through October 22. The exhibition consisted of thirty-seven ink and wash drawings executed between 1927 and 1928, allegedly based on sketches dating back to 1917.[26] Orozco wrote Charlot:

> The serious thing is that an exhibition has been arranged of the already famous "horrors" in one of the most "exclusive" galleries of 57th Street, the Marie Sterner, together with other exhibitions of 6 French [artists], Matisse and others. This exhibition is as good as an introduction to the upper circles of painting.[27]

To his wife he wrote:

> Love, last night I visited Alma Reed and she gave me a series of FANTASTIC news! The first is that I will have the first exhibition of my work at the Marie Sterner gallery, which is one of the most exclusive.[28]

Much to the disappointment of Reed and Orozco, the exhibition received no critical notice, and not a single work was sold.[29]

Orozco was becoming increasingly close to Reed and

Sikelianos, going with them everywhere and visiting their apartment several times a week. He shared this with his wife, Margarita, writing to her, "Both Alma and Mrs. Sikelianos are behaving towards me in the most generous and courteous manner, you have no idea, as if I was in reality their son."[30] Margarita did not react favorably to this closeness, and she must have expressed her concern to Orozco in letters (he destroyed her letters to him before he returned to Mexico in 1934). He responded in November:

> Your last two letters made me sad for various reasons, I see that you have formed a wrong idea regarding my dealings with Mrs. Sikelianos and Alma Reed. It is true that they esteem and care for me greatly, but it does not go beyond the purely intellectual plane, professional.[31]

In the same letter, Orozco assesses his artistic prospects realistically yet also with optimism. He writes of the possibility of painting portraits but discards this possibility both for lack of a proper studio and no real interest in this very society-connected genre. He mentions the different annual exhibitions, though he acknowledges that the chances of making a living by selling work through the annuals is remote. Finally, he brings up murals and the possibility of getting commissions through publicity and dropping off photographic portfolios at architectural firms. While Orozco waited, Reed became more involved as a champion of his talent, and Sikelianos returned to Greece.[32]

Throughout this period, Orozco corresponded with Charlot, with whom he shares visual experiences. He wonders whether Georges Rouault was familiar with Mexican Holy Week imagery; he visits an exhibition of Spanish painting at the Metropolitan Museum, where he sees Velázquez and Goya, but he is most impressed by El Greco, whom he considers God. He does not like Forain and finds Renoir weak after the third encounter.[33]

Orozco's first encounter with Seurat was profound:

> The first Seurat that I see; he must have been a man of simplicity and pure heart, one feels guilty and filled with sin in front of his painting filled with light, the

other pictures seem dirty, even Cézanne, even Renoir;
if there was a need (and there isn't one) for religious
painting, it would be—Seurat—and not the ugly
monkeys that are placed on altars.[34]

The clarity and order of Seurat obviously impressed
Orozco, who himself thought of composition as the true
basis of picture-making. Seurat often used the golden section (the proportion and relation between the minor and
major side of a rectangle) as the basis of his compositions;
no doubt this was a factor in Orozco's admiration. In this
context, it is important to recall Orozco's earlier impression of American painters:

> I assure you it is quite a tragedy that of the Ameri-
> can painters. . . . The true american artists are those
> who make the machines: in front of them one must
> discover oneself.[35]

Given this statement, one wonders how Orozco would
have reacted to the work of the precisionists. They were,
after all, painting machines in a machinelike manner.
Orozco possibly saw works by the leading precisionists at
the Downtown Gallery, but if he did, his opinion has never
been documented.

Edith Halpert of the Downtown Gallery showed an
early interest in Orozco's work. She handled some of his
lithographs at the end of 1928, selling six of them at $13
each.[36] She also gave Orozco a three-week exhibition of
easel paintings of New York scenes, which opened on
March 26, 1929.[37] Orozco complained to Charlot in February that he still had not finished the pictures that were
to be exhibited at the Downtown Gallery.[38] Paintings of
1928 and early 1929, such as *Eighth Avenue, The Subway,
Fourteenth Street, Manhattan,* and *The Elevated,* were in the
exhibition. *The Subway* was acquired by Abigail Aldrich
Rockefeller, a regular client of the gallery.[39]

In January 1929, Orozco wrote and published a
short article in the magazine *Creative Art* that presented
his aesthetic credo. Entitled "New World, New Races, and
New Art," it stated:

The art of the New World cannot take root in the old traditions of the Old World nor in aboriginal traditions represented by the remains of our ancient indian peoples, although the art of all races and of all times has a common value—human, universal—each new cycle must work for itself, must create, must yield its own production, its individual share to the common good. To go solicitously to Europe, bent on poking about its ruins in order to import them and servilely to copy them, is no greater error than is the looting of the indigenous remains of the New World with the object of copying with equal servility its ruins or its present folklore. However picturesque and interesting these may be, however reproductive and useful ethnology may find them, they cannot furnish a point of departure for the new creation. To lean upon the art of the aborigines, whether it be of antiquity or of the present day, is a sure indication of impotence and cowardice, in fact, of fraud.

If *new* races have appeared upon the land of the *New World*, such races have the unavoidable duty to produce a *New Art* in a new spiritual and physical medium. Any other road is plain cowardice.

Already, the architecture of Manhattan is a new value, something that has nothing to do with Egyptian pyramids, with the Paris Opera, with the Giralda of Seville, or with Saint Sophia, any more than it has to do with the Maya palaces of Chicen Itza or with the "Pueblos" of Arizona. Imagine the New York Stock Exchange in a french cathedral. Imagine the brokers all rigged out like indian chieftains, with head feathers or with mexican sombreros. The architecture of Manhattan is the first step. Painting and sculpture must certainly follow as inevitable second steps.

The highest, the most logical, the purest and strongest form of painting is the mural. In this form alone, it is one with the other arts—with all the others.

It is too, the most disinterested form, for it

cannot be made for private gain; it cannot be hidden away for the benefit of a certain privileged few. It is for the people. It is for *ALL*.[40]

In this brief article Orozco made clear his position: he advocated the creation of a new art that was dependent neither on Europe nor the indigenous past of the Americas. As a new, hybrid people in a new world, the artists of the Americas had a duty to create a new art. Orozco celebrated the architecture of Manhattan as an example of the new art, even though over time he would become increasingly ambiguous about the newness and beauty of New York City's skyscrapers. Unlike Rivera, who acknowledged the living presence of indigenous cultures, Orozco, as is evident in this article, saw them as part of the past. What is abundantly clear is his idealistic belief in the unique importance of mural painting as the strongest form of painting for that time and place.

During February 1929, Orozco's work left the boundaries of New York City when he presented a small group of easel pictures at The Little Gallery in Philadelphia. Organized by Mary Collum, the gallery's director, the exhibition had been the idea of painter George Biddle, who had met Orozco through Walter Pach. Biddle even made introductory remarks at the opening of the exhibition, and his brother, Francis, future attorney general under Roosevelt, acquired the painting *Coney Island Side Show* for $150.[41]

Throughout the first two weeks of April, preparatory sketches for the Preparatoria murals, along with photographs of them by Tina Modotti, were exhibited at the Architectural League of New York.[42] During the preparations for this exhibition, Orozco met Thomas Hart Benton:

T. Benton, a good painter who could become a caricature of himself, teaches at the "Art Students League" and has invited me to exhibit drawings, lithographs and paintings in the large gallery there. He is enthusiastic about my mural work, and has the golden dream of painting large decorations in buildings. He sends large canvases to the League of Architects every year, but so far has not been able to secure even one commission. He makes a living by being a teacher at the Academy.[43]

On April 15, Orozco's exhibition opened at the Art Students League. The exhibition had an impact not just on the students but also on the faculty. Will Barnet, who came to the league the following year to study lithography, recalled the impact:

> I arrived at the League a year after Orozco had exhibited there, yet the students and faculty were still talking of the monumental forms, the sober drama of the content . . . everyone wanted to paint murals.[44]

The exhibition at the league was up for two weeks. During this time, Orozco wrote to Margarita:

> [W]hen I arrive at the school they treat me with a great deal of respect and many attentions. Truly, they have behaved well towards me. A student told me that after seeing my works he wanted to throw out the window everything of his, and one of the most popular american painters, Mr. J. Sloan, said that this was one of the best exhibits of paintings he had seen in New York in many a year, including the exhibitions that you pay a dollar to get in.[45]

As early as February of the previous year, Orozco had started executing lithographs with the printer George Miller, who had a shop on Fourteenth Street and printed for artists associated with the Weyhe Gallery.[46] Orozco's correspondence with both Charlot and Margarita is filled with his skeptical remarks regarding "old man" Erhard Weyhe and his establishment.

In June 1929, Alma Reed arranged for an exhibition of drawings and small easel paintings at the Chicago Arts Club.[47] The exhibition opened on June 15 and closed on the 29.[48] Orozco wrote Margarita:

> My exhibition at the Arts Club is very fine and yesterday they gave me a good reception which was attended by many people. The exhibition of the "Century of Progress" is no big deal. They have

there a ridiculous "Mexican Village," but it is very
popular. From Mexico they are sending lots of
knick knacks to sell.[49]

In the same letter Orozco describes how much Reed
has helped him while complaining of how tired he is of
the insecurity of his lifestyle. Yet he stresses to Margarita
that there is no other way to achieve a name for himself
and that they must all be patient.[50] A week and a half later
Orozco returned to Mexico to spend the entire summer
with his family.[51] This is the only occasion when he returned to his homeland during his stay in the United States
from 1927 through 1934. Before going back to Mexico,
Orozco and Reed came to an understanding regarding the
promotion of his career. When he returned to New York
in September, she would become his full-time representative and possibly open a gallery devoted to his work.[52]

By the summer of 1929, Orozco's name was beginning to circulate in the New York City art world. Although
he was still looking for walls on which to execute murals,
his drawings, prints, and easel paintings were being seen
and noticed. His early period of isolation was definitely at
an end. In Alma Reed he had acquired an advocate for the
work he wanted to do in Gringoland.

The Delphic Studios

One of the difficulties in re-creating the exhibitions that
took place at the Delphic Studios is the lack of archival
materials for the gallery. When Alma Reed died in Mexico
in 1961, the apartment where she was living was cleaned
out, and all of her papers, including the Delphic Studios
records, disappeared.[53]

After spending the summer of 1929 in Mexico with
his wife and three children, Orozco was back in New York
City by September 8. He wrote to Margarita:

> Adored Little wife: I am still tired from the trip, this
> time I got very tired and I could barely sleep during
> the four nights, so you can imagine how worn out
> and without desire to do anything I am. I am in-
> stalled in an "apartment" which Alma found for me

and fixed, it is well situated and comfortable, it has a large room with two windows to the street and a small bedroom with windows to the street. Also there is a bathroom, closets and a small kitchen of about one square meter, but with all the necessities. The "apartment" costs 70 dol. a month and I have taken it for ten months. Really it is not possible to find any better in N. York for what I need and my possibilities. You must suppose how much I miss you and I miss the little ones, I hope that some day you will become aware of how much it is my share to suffer, no matter whether or not you believe that "he who leaves" does not suffer.[54]

Orozco settled in at 46 West Fiftieth Street and started getting ready for the upcoming exhibition season. He was still not making much money, yet his name and work were starting to be recognized.

The Delphic Studios, located at 9 East Fifty-seventh Street, opened its doors on October 14, 1929. The gallery consisted of two large and two small rooms. The opening exhibition featured drawings by Thomas Hart Benton spread out between one large and one small room. One small room decorated in a Greek style contained Chinese furniture, Byzantine icons, and Persian rugs, which were for sale. The last large room had a number of Orozco's easel paintings and lithographs on permanent display.[55] The lithographs were without a doubt the seven that Orozco had executed up to that time at George Miller's shop on Fourteenth Street: *Vaudeville in Harlem*, *Bandera*, *Requiem*, *Casa arruinada*, *Soldados Mexicanos*, *Revolución*, and *Retaguardia*. Since no checklist exists for the exhibition, we have no idea which easel paintings were exhibited. It is possible that, with the exception of one lithograph, all of the works were of Mexican subjects.

During the days prior to the opening of the Delphic Studios, Orozco received a visit from Antonieta Rivas Mercado (1900–1931), an occasional journalist, patron of the painter Manuel Rodríguez Lozano (1898–1970), and lover of José Vasconcelos. Rodríguez Lozano was an easel painter with a

decidedly antinationalist and antimuralist position. His paintings reflect the influence of Picasso's neoclassical period,
charged with Rodríguez Lozano's own homoeroticism.
Orozco helped Rivas Mercado find a place to stay (at the
YWCA), yet avoided her as much as possible. He found her
unstable, obsessed with the painter Rodríguez Lozano, and
constantly campaigning for Vasconcelos, who would lose the
1929 Mexican presidential election.[56]

Rivas Mercado, in turn, wrote to Rodríguez Lozano
giving her impression of Orozco and Reed:

> My dear Manuel, I move on to Clemente. We just
> finished with the case of Diego and now, you'll be
> the judge, we must move on to the case of
> Clemente. Who can resist that everyday they burn
> the incense of one's genius? Alma Reed is an
> Antonieta that would not have known Rodríguez
> Lozano, all good will and disorientation. Alma,
> who is well connected, weaves with red thread her
> tragedy with Carrillo Puerto and because of this,
> has a great interest in Mexico. Clemente, a Mexi-
> can, unprotected and with genius gave her the re-
> venge over Mexico, which killed her Carrillo eight
> days before the wedding. She has adopted him and
> for 3 or 5 days does not do anything but create a
> reputation for Orozco in the U.S. Articles, exhibi-
> tions, lectures, etc. Finally she has taken a place on
> 57 Street, where all the best art galleries are, half a
> block from Fifth Avenue, where she has opened a
> gallery dedicated to Orozco. She currently has up
> drawings by a horrible gringo painter. In two years
> time Orozco will be rich and famous. He thinks
> he is really something, painting easel pictures in
> eight hours or in a day. Not once, but several times,
> I have said to Alma, in front of him, that when no
> one did him justice in Mexico, you were the only
> one to defend him—Clemente has forgotten and
> when I have said it he does not continue the con-
> versation. But no, he follows the tactic of that pig
> Diego, how grave to be like your enemies! I will

start my campaign on your behalf, of Abraham and
Julio, and Clemente will not like it.[57]

Rivas Mercado views Orozco as an artist full of himself and secure in the aesthetic value of his works. She sees
Reed as naive and totally taken in by him. In Orozco's
correspondence with his wife, however, he is always re-
strained in his assessment of himself and his paintings,
while Reed comes across as the bold muse who is willing
to try anything in order to promote the artist.

In his 1969 autobiography, Benton recalled the genesis
of the Delphic Studios:

> The Delphic Gallery was founded by Alma Reed who,
> as a buxom and attractive blonde reporter had found
> herself in Mexico. . . . Alma envisaged a resuscitation
> of the Greek mysteries of Delphi in a new and mod-
> ern form. This was too esoteric for me, but because
> Alma had the Mexican painter Clemente Orozco in
> tow and because I had great admiration for his work,
> I joined her organization.[58]

According to Orozco's correspondence, the opening
of the Delphic Studios was well attended by the leading
lights of the New York art world, and yet once again the
art magazines did not carry a single mention of it. Orozco's
own recollection of the Delphic Studios in his autobiography is brief and humorous:

> Once Delphic Studios opened to the public, there
> came some white Russians who had fled Moscow
> on the triumph of the bolshevik revolution, and had
> gone through Shanghai and San Francisco, end-
> ing their long trip in New York. They bought an
> enormous number of art objects whose sale they
> proposed. They had icons beautifully covered in
> gold and silver. Chinese paintings, furniture and
> pots of incredible sumptuousness, ancient Persian
> tapestries of all sizes, and fantastic drawings, rare
> porcelains, ivories; and to complete these wonders,
> some objects that had been the personal property
> of the last Czar of Russia, Nicholas II. Among these

objects there was a monumental table clock, about
a meter high, given to the czar by his relatives on
one of his birthdays, according to a large inscrip-
tion with the names of the archdukes and archduch-
esses. The clock was mounted on a solid silver base
and on the base there was a playful infinity of fat
little angels doing a thousand cute and mischievous
things. The totality was heavy, insolent and of bad
taste. All of the objects of the collection found their
way slowly towards museums and private collections,
but the czar's clock would not sell. I had it in my
bedroom for a long time and it kept me company
until Los Angeles where I lost sight of it.[59]

Orozco devotes barely a page to the Delphic Studios
in his entire autobiography, written eleven years after he
left New York in 1934. The passage reflects the end of his
relationship with Reed, his insistence upon downplaying
the importance of the Delphic Studios in promoting his
work, and perhaps also a way of pleasing his wife by not
giving much importance to an enterprise headed by Reed.
Orozco's correspondence with his wife from September
1928 through May 1932 is filled with constant references
to Alma Reed and her plans for promoting his work. On a
number of occasions, Margarita must have expressed concerns regarding Reed's attitude toward the artist and his
art. Orozco would always write back assuring her of his
love and reassuring her that nothing was going on between
himself and his patron. He insisted that theirs was a purely
professional relationship. Despite Orozco's denials to his
wife, however, many rumors have surfaced over the years
of an affair between the artist and his dealer.[60]

The Delphic Studios promoted Orozco in a consistent
manner. In looking at the *Art Index* for the years 1929
through 1935, one finds thirty-nine entries for Orozco reviews and articles and eighteen reproductions. Some of
these appeared in the major art periodicals of the time,
such as *Creative Art, Art News*, and *London Studio*. When the
Delphic Studios opened in October, 1929, the economic
crash that ushered in the Depression occurred at the end of

that month, affecting every facet of life in the country, including the arts. On February 3, 1930, the Delphic Studios inaugurated a second exhibition of Orozco's recent paintings and gouaches, which remained open until February 25. After this exhibition, the gallery would no longer present Orozco's work in the form of a one-man show. Instead, it would display the work in a quasi-permanent installation, which would change whenever the artist finished new pieces.[61] Reed would continue to exhibit and sell work by Benton, Boardman Robinson, Miguel Covarrubias, and Fidelio Ponce, along with work by Orozco.[62]

According to the artist's family, Reed's failure as a dealer of Orozco's work is explained by the fact that, as Orozco was becoming better known, his prices were not increasing but decreasing.[63] This fact cannot be substantiated by checking the sales records of the Delphic Studios, because they are no longer in existence. During the early 1930s, due to the Depression, all art prices fell. Moreover, it is true that collector Dr. Alvar Carillo Gil was able to acquire many of Orozco's works from the 1929–32 period for a modest sum during the 1940s.[64] As an art dealer, Reed is remembered by those who knew her as very attractive, articulate, and aggressive, but also as someone who was forced to improvise as she went along. She was not, for instance, a professional like Edith Halpert.[65] Again, it is important to be aware that shortly after the Delphic Studios opened its doors, the stock market crash ushered in the Depression. This socioeconomic situation not only had a devastating effect on an already debilitated art world, but, most importantly, it affected the entire nation. In the cities the unemployed were in the streets, while in the southern and western regions of the country racism and lynchings became more rampant. This crisis situation would be evoked, directly and indirectly, in Orozco's paintings and graphic works of his New York period.

It was through Reed and the Delphic Studios that Orozco came in contact with Stephen C. Clark and Frank Lloyd Wright. Clark was a prominent collector and trustee of The Museum of Modern Art, which had opened its doors in November 1929. Wright at this time was something of a "has been"; earlier he had been the leading architect in the United States and a very controversial person as well. Orozco wrote Margarita in a letter of May 1931:

> Clark came early this morning and he liked very much the paintings I am doing. . . . He told Alma that I am one of the greatest artists of today. . . . He says that what I need now is to paint large and very important paintings in order to have an exhibition at The Museum of Modern Art. He will buy five or six at the price of $2,500 each for his own collection, which later on will be given to the museum.[66]

In the same letter, Orozco relates how well he got along with Clark, as well as how important The Museum of Modern Art was in the presentation of contemporary art. He mentions that Rivera would be having a retrospective there at the end of the year and that this was due to Alfred H. Barr Jr., the director. He proceeds to write a tirade against the "Mastodon" (Rivera) and to say that Barr saw him (Orozco) as a savage who painted badly.[67]

Career-wise, the contact with Clark was an important boost for Orozco, and he continued to mention Clark's visits to the Delphic Studios in the correspondence with his wife during the summer of 1931. Still, Clark was unable to convince Barr to give Orozco an exhibition at the museum. The closest the artist would come to anything like a major venue was in 1940 when he painted the portable mural *Dive Bomber and Tank*.

In 1932, long after Orozco had finished the New School mural, Frank Lloyd Wright visited the institution and then sought out the artist at the Delphic Studios. Orozco wrote Margarita of the visit:

> The well known architect F. Lloyd Wright came to the gallery after visiting the New School and seeing my murals there. He told me I am a master painter and that he wants me to work for him. He will bring you and the children, build a studio for me in Wisconsin . . . it is something to think about.[68]

Reed recalled the words of Wright in her 1956 biography of the artist:

José Orozco, you are an authentic master. At last, I find in you a painter with whom I wish to collaborate on great projects. I am willing to form an exclusive working partnership with you for the rest of our days. Never before in history have an architect and a painter of our ability and our vision had the good fortune to create and execute together. Let us take advantage of the unique circumstances for the enrichment of contemporary art and life.[69]

Undoubtedly, Reed has embellished Wright's words with the passage of time and her sense of the "momentousness" of the encounter. Yet the meeting did take place, and Orozco was made an incredible offer for that time.

By 1932 Frank Lloyd Wright had completed the Larkin Administration Building (1906), Unity Temple (1906), the Robie House (1909), and the Imperial Hotel in Tokyo (1922), but he was not building and instead was preoccupied with city planning and the establishment of Taliesin. Ahead of him were Fallingwater (1936) and the Johnson Wax buildings (1938 and 1948), and the writing of three books on architecture. He would establish the Taliesin Fellowship in Wisconsin in 1932, and he must have foreseen Orozco's playing a role there. Orozco reacted cautiously, however. After thinking about the offer for several days, he decided against it. Orozco knew an egoist when he met one and he became wary. Years later he told his son, Alfredo, also an architect, that Wright thought architecture the greatest of all arts and that under the shadow of such a large tree, nothing could grow.[70] Decorative murals in some of Wright's Prairie School houses are more abstract than realistic. Wright must have responded to the abstract patterns and monochromatic qualities of Orozco's work. Since Wright was at a critical point in his career, he perhaps thought Orozco would be a boost to his architectural enterprise. Orozco's independent spirit was reaffirmed by his response to Wright's offer, and this at a time when the artist badly needed economic stability. Orozco was not just cautious but also practical, since he realized that Wright was out of work.

Reed would always blame the October 1929 crash for

the lack of economic success of the Delphic Studios in general and of Orozco's work in particular. Again, the absence of existing records makes it impossible to evaluate the evolution, or lack of it, in Orozco sales during the height of the Delphic Studios (1929–34). By May 1931, Orozco started to complain in letters to his wife of Reed's 50-percent cut on all sales, of her practice of giving works away to make "important contacts," and of the lack of clear records for any transactions occurring at the gallery.[71]

The year 1932 saw the publication by the Delphic Studios of Reed's *José Clemente Orozco*. It is believed that Reed herself paid for the printing of the book. This in itself sheds light on the nature of their relationship; an outlay of this order on the part of the dealer was more than a business deal. The first monograph on the artist, the book contained an introduction by the author, a one-page biographical chronology by Orozco, and more than two hundred black-and-white reproductions of murals, easel paintings, prints, and drawings. The photographs of the Preparatoria murals in the book had been taken by Tina Modotti in 1926 and 1927. It is believed that many of the early drawings and paintings reproduced in the book had been given earlier (and also false) dates by Reed, presumably with Orozco's approval. This was part of Reed's plan to prove that Orozco had depicted certain Mexican themes earlier than Rivera.[72] Concerning the book, *The Art Digest* stated: "Miss Reed has brought out a valuable work and a timely one."[73] The book was sold at the Delphic Studios and the Weyhe Gallery in New York, while in Mexico City it was carried by the Libreria Misrachi.[74]

By the time Orozco finished the frescoes at Dartmouth College in February 1934, his business relationship with Reed and the Delphic Studios was strained. When he returned to Mexico in June, he no longer considered Reed his exclusive representative.[75]

Orozco came back to New York in February 1936 to address the first American Artists Congress as a representative of Liga de Escritores y Artistas Revolucionarios (LEAR), an antifascist front organization of Mexican artists (more on his address appears in chapter 5). In his correspondence to

Margarita, he claims not to have seen Reed during this visit. When he returned in May 1940 to paint *Dive Bomber and Tank* for The Museum of Modern Art, Reed sought him out at his hotel. Again, Orozco's version to Margarita was that he was short with her, and she went on her way.[76] The Delphic Studios had finally closed its doors the previous month.[77] Without a doubt, between 1929 and 1934 Alma Reed helped Orozco make a name for himself in Gringoland. During this time, the Delphic Studios was *the* Orozco gallery. Even after the artist's death, Reed would not give up that easily on Orozco as *her* subject; in 1956, seven years after Orozco's death, she would publish a biography of him containing twenty chapters and 308 pages. Of these, pages 29 through 271 are dedicated to his seven years in New York. The years from 1934 through 1949 are covered in only 36 pages. Clearly, the author is giving importance to the years spent by the artist with her in New York City.[78]

The other important event in Orozco's artistic education during his New York City years was his only visit to Europe during the summer months of 1932. Orozco devotes five pages to this trip in his autobiography. He states that he went only to see some of the great paintings in museums and churches. He first visited London, where he was quite taken with both the clarity and colors of Raphael's cartoons at the Victoria and Albert Museum. He found the capital of the British Empire shabby, dirty, and full of beggars: "I could never have imagined that I, a citizen of a modest country, 'semi-colonial' as they say, would be giving coins to the hungry in the streets and squares of the English capital."[79] Paris he considered to be old, miserable, and filled with transvestites. Although he saw a "great" retrospective exhibition of Picasso at the Georges Petit gallery, he was also keenly aware of the havoc being wrought by fascism in Europe.[80]

Throughout Europe, from England to Spain, El Greco made the most profound impact upon Orozco; his mannerist color, rough application of pigment, and agitated draftsmanship were studied and absorbed. In Toledo, Orozco found that "they still bury the Count of Orgaz, El Greco lives there, painting, and his apostles work daily. One brings my luggage to the hotel, another one serves me a glass of wine, the one over there is the driver on the bus to Madrid and I see another one on the bridge of Alcántara."[81]

Orozco was forty-nine years old when he went to Europe. As an artist he had been essentially formed by then, so he was simply double-checking works that he previously had known either through reproductions or word of mouth. Orozco had no great epiphany in the Old World. For Rivera, Europe was a laboratory for experimenting in painting that lasted fourteen years. Not so for Orozco—a man who hated tourists yet nonetheless went to Europe as a tourist to view the marvels of Western painting. In his own words, his return trip allowed six days of perfect rest on the Atlantic Ocean, and then he was in New York.[82] Always there was New York, that amusement park/monstrosity where he felt both alien and at home.

EASEL PAINTINGS, DRAWINGS, AND LITHOGRAPHS, 1928-32

Orozco's one public definition of painting, written in 1940, states:

> A painting is a Poem and nothing else. A poem made of relationships between forms as other kinds of poems are made of relationships between words, sounds or ideas. Sculpture and architecture are also relationships between forms. This word forms includes color, tone, proportion, line, etcetera.[1]

Earlier, in responding to Alma Reed's question, "What is art?," Orozco said, "Art is knowledge at the service of emotion."[2] It is worthwhile to note the formal aspect of these statements, considering they were made by an expressionistic and politically engaged painter. Orozco's easel paintings have generally been relegated to secondary status due to his importance as a muralist. There is no doubt as to the superiority of most of the murals, yet this should not take away from the importance of some of his easel pictures. At times, the easel pictures served as laboratories for ideas and forms to be expressed later on a larger scale. Most of the time, they stand as works that begin and end within themselves. A great many of the easel pictures are failures. When they are complete as pictorial statements, they achieve the visual and emotional vigor of his best murals. Even the unresolved pictures tell us much of the artist's view of modernity as expressed through New York City, particularly when we compare his subjects with similar subjects painted by artists like the precisionists and the Fourteenth Street School. His Mexican subjects among these easel pictures are complex and tragic, radically different from the subjects chosen by Rivera and others.

After reviewing the general (and incomplete) registry of Orozco's easel work at the Carillo Gil Museum and noting the various works mentioned in the artist's correspondence as well as those reproduced during the years 1929–34, I have identified a total of forty-four works painted in New York City. These can be divided into four categories: New York scenes, Mexican scenes, mythological (Greek-inspired) or surreal subjects, and portraits. Of these four categories, the most interesting and fully realized pictures are among the New York and Mexican scenes.[3]

Orozco painted these easel pictures usually in his living quarters, although after meeting Eva Sikelianos and Alma Reed, he did set up a kind of temporary studio in their apartment at the south end of the living room: "Each day after painting, Orozco would carefully remove the easel and other equipment to a room at the rear of the apartment which he had dubbed the pulquería."[4] After the Delphic Studios opened, Orozco continued to paint in the apartment he was occupying at the time, in the gallery itself, and from April 1931 through March 1932 in a small skylight duplex on West Forty-fourth Street that he shared with his wife and children, who were visiting at this time.

Everywhere he worked, his needs were similar to what they would be for the rest of his life. Orozco's studios during the 1930s and 1940s in both Guadalajara and Mexico City were spare and orderly, containing no more than one or two easels, a drawing table for the execution of works on paper, brushes, pencils, and other supplies.[5] Throughout the

1930s, Orozco's stark palette in oils consisted of the colors zinc white, ivory black, viridian, cadmium red, burnt sienna, india brown, mars ocher, cobalt blue, and ultramarine blue. Orozco preferred to paint with bristle brushes and to mix his colors with a combination of half turpentine, a quarter linseed oil, and a quarter varnish.[6] Orozco painted on either coarse cotton or duck canvas, which he primed with a mixture of zinc white, whiting, and linseed oil.[7] Based on the artist's correspondence with his wife, as well as the abundant seals on stretchers and notebooks, it is evident that Orozco purchased most of his materials and had pieces framed at Schneider & Co., Inc., Artists Materials Exclusively, located at 123 West Sixty-eighth Street.[8]

Orozco's earliest New York period paintings range in size from small, such as *Coney Island*, 9 5/8 by 8 1/8 inches, to medium, such as *Queensborough Bridge*, 19 by 24 inches. The two sizes used most by the artist until 1931 were 19 1/2 by 24 inches and 24 by 30 inches. In 1931, at the suggestion of Stephen C. Clark, Orozco started painting large easel pictures, using canvases with the dimensions of 45 by 55 inches.

New York Scenes

We know from his autobiography that Orozco took long walks along Riverside Drive, by the Hudson River, and around Columbia University. He would also travel by subway to the other end of the island, Little Italy, and the Lower East Side; visit composer Carlos Chávez in Greenwich Village; and "in two minutes go from Italy to China and Japan." He became thoroughly familiar with the city and its surrounding boroughs, and he traveled by subway even though he was not a fan of the invention. Orozco called New York an "imperial city" in his autobiography. In a letter to Margarita, he described it as "part amusement park and part growing monstrosity."[9] The city, which extracted ambiguous responses from him, would be the subject of nineteen easel paintings. Only six in this group are truly successful works in both form and content, while the rest are interesting by what they propose yet fail to achieve.

As he had during his first visit, Orozco visited Coney Island, writing:

Those who speak of large multitudes and mass meetings without seeing Coney Island on a Sunday in the summer do not know what they are talking about. . . . It is precisely at night when marvelous and great things happen, as Coney Island lights up with the lights of artificial fireworks.

Along the beach, there is a great fair, typically American, with many attractions. . . . One must mention the bearded woman, the fattest woman in the world, the ape man, the one with two heads, the dwarfs, the half-man, half-woman and other freaks.[10]

As far as we know, Orozco's first New York easel picture, *Coney Island Side Show* (1928; fig. 9), is an indirect reflection of this experience. Measuring less than ten by nine inches, it is the smallest oil executed by the artist. A dark and compressed picture comprised of browns, blacks, pinks, and oranges, it represents a night scene. Yet the artist does not depict in it any of the freaks he mentions. Instead, we see a scantily clothed woman, her arms outstretched. Her face is defined by seven quickly drawn lines that give her features. Behind her is a male figure with a grotesque face, a torso covered with spots (perhaps he is the leopard man?), and no hands. Behind them are either billboards whose letters we cannot see or curtains that cover the entrance to a tent. At their feet, we see the backs of the audience, some of whom are female bathers. There is an oppressive quality to this picture, created in part by the dark palette and thickly applied colors, as well as by the compression of foreground, middle ground, and background. The two figures on the stage live on the fringes of society; they have a kinship with the beggars and prostitutes of Orozco's earlier work (1913–17). This is definitely not the Coney Island of painters like John Sloan, Reginald Marsh, or Paul Cadmus, a place filled with fleshy, animalistic sexuality, painted satirically "from above." Rather, it is a place of strangers seen by an outsider. Orozco is not part of the sideshow, yet neither does he belong in the audience. His viewpoint is suspended between the two. Orozco's only experience of crowds was during the Mexican Revolution;

these were either what he witnessed while with the Red Battalions or at meetings at the Casa del Obrero Mundial. They were political and chaotic crowds, but still premodern Mexican ones. It was in New York and places like Coney Island where he encountered the modern, urban, thoroughly anonymous, even alienated crowd.

A contemporary of Orozco who had a similar experience with New York was the Spanish poet Federico García Lorca (1898–1936). García Lorca was in New York City in 1929–30, studying English at Columbia University. At this time, he met Orozco through the Spanish painter and critic Gabriel García Maroto.[11] The poet responded to Coney Island by writing the poem *Landscape of a Vomiting Multitude (Dusk at Coney Island)*, a hallucinogenic piece filled with grotesque and surreal elements, while Orozco responded to the same environment by painting a physically small picture of a minute fragment of the crowd.[12] Like Orozco, García Lorca came from an essentially presecular and agrarian nation. Like the Mexican painter, the Andalusian poet was a leftist of sorts. Orozco came from anarchosyndicalism, and García Lorca

FIG. 9: *Coney Island Side Show*, 1928, oil on canvas. Private collection.

was becoming a fellow-traveler of the Spanish Communist Party. Both experienced a place like Coney Island with awe and revulsion. As stated earlier, there is also a possible connection with Baudelaire's sense of the modern as tied to the grotesque and marginal. It is possible that both the Mexican painter and the Spanish poet were aware of the French author's ideas on this subject.

Subways have been depicted by American painters

throughout the twentieth century. The artists who worked around Fourteenth Street and Union Square, however, made them a central subject of their art. Kenneth Hayes Miller, Reginald Marsh, Isabel Bishop, Raphael Soyer, and others rejected modernism in favor of a realistic depiction of modern life within a narrative context. The first three of these artists even looked to the Renaissance and baroque periods for stylistic inspiration. They all had studios in or around Union Square, and their paintings depicted the life on Fourteenth Street. When they painted the subway, it was usually as a modern means of transportation where characters from all walks of life would cross each other's paths. Miller's subway paintings depict middle-aged matrons carrying bags, while Marsh mixed voluptuous young women with derelicts. Bishop portrayed mothers with exhausted children, and Soyer, tired clerical workers of both genders. In general, these paintings depict the "new woman" who has left home to do her own shopping or, better yet, earn her own living.[13] Orozco's single depiction of a subway is an entirely different matter. Entitled *The Subway* (fig. 10) and painted the same year as *Coney Island Side Show*, it is a larger painting, measuring 16 by 21 3/8 inches. A horizontal composition, the painting's overall tone is dark. Orozco composes a series of austere rectangles and curves formed by the windows, seats, and bars. Comprised of mostly umbers and ochers, there are touches of viridian and orange to accentuate the earth colors. The three figures, all males, are massive and dark. They wear hats and have their backs turned to each other. Their faces are quick, masklike sketches that lack individuality. The bodies of these men disappear under their heavy coats. They inhabit the same space yet are emotionally separate. This is a somber and claustrophobic painting, reflecting Orozco's dislike of underground trains. In *The Subway*, the men keep to themselves, behind their painted masks. This painting is definitely the antithesis of the paintings of the Fourteenth Street School of the same subject, which are usually full of movement and sensuality. These passengers are automatons, stuck in a mechanical contraption that transports them underneath a world of sunlight.

FIG. 10: *The Subway*, 1928, oil on paper laid down on board. Private collection.

According to Gail Stavitsky, precisionism was not a coherent movement with a program. Its stylistic sources lay in the paintings made by European artists like Francis Picabia and Marcel Duchamp when they were in New York City during World War I. These painters' subject matter tended to be mostly industrial, even if not all of the subjects were urban. They responded to forms within the environment but rarely to the environment itself.[14] The paintings of precisionist artists can be cold, very much enamored of the industrial forms that are being depicted. As an avid gallery goer, Orozco must have encountered while in New York the work of these artists, whether at Stieglitz's or the Downtown and Daniel galleries. The aesthetic of precisionism was a part of a sensibility that was "in the air," brought about to a degree by the implementation of mass production and the prosperity of the 1920s.

A painting of Orozco's that reflects this milieu is the 1928 *New York Factory, Williamsburg* (fig. 11), an oil on canvas measuring roughly twenty-eight by nineteen inches. Coarsely painted, it represents five buildings with three massive chimneys. As in a typical precisionist picture, there are no figures present, but the similarity stops there. These are not beautiful industrial forms; instead, they are heavy boxes painted in sienna, black, and crimson. The sky is a yellow ocher with patches of dirty pink. The massive brown chimney in the foreground spews a dark gray-green smoke into the sky. We do not know if it is dawn or dusk. Orozco paints the reality generally ignored by the precisionists: the harshness and brutality of a factory. There are no beautiful forms here. Once again, García Lorca in words crosses paths with Orozco:

> As I said to you I was friendly with Clemente Orozco these past nine months in New York. In the last years, he has painted some small and horrible pictures of the environments of the city. I remember one of a factory, which he painted like a dark jail, not a soul in the streets.[15]

If we compare Orozco's painting of a factory with any work by Charles Demuth or Charles Sheeler, leading precisionists, the differences are radical. A Demuth painting usually has bright colors and clear outlines, and the industrial shapes are depicted with a classical aesthetic. Works such as these are about order and serenity. *New York Factory, Williamsburg* is about an oppressive kind of solitude. We do not see what goes on inside the buildings, yet their dark, heavy exterior reflects pessimism.

The elevated trains were another part of New York City since the start of the twentieth century. Painters like John Sloan, John Marin, and Edward Hopper used this subject in their work. So, too, did the precisionist painters and the artists of the Fourteenth Street School. Orozco painted two versions of the El, one larger and sketchlike, dated 1928 (Carillo Gil Museum), and a smaller version from the same year (private collection, Mexico City). The latter is the fully realized picture in the most formal sense. Entitled *The Third Avenue Elevated* (fig. 12), it is an oil on canvas mounted on masonite, measuring roughly twenty by thirty-four inches. This painting focuses on the mechanical structure of the elevated station on Third Avenue.

FIG. 11: *New York Factory, Williamsburg,* 1928, oil on canvas. Private collection. (facing page)

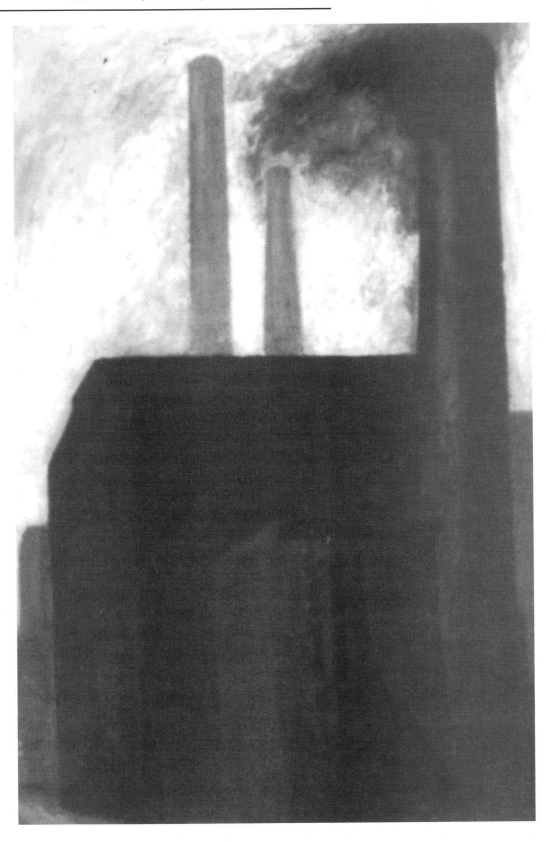

FIG. 12: *The Third Avenue Elevated,*
1928, oil on canvas.
Private collection.

Painted in brown, ocher, and green, the work depicts an
entrance to the station. On either side of the central structure, Orozco painted the staircases with their peaked roofs.
Orozco's encounters with cubism in the New York galleries is evident in this work; we can see this in the geometric
and juxtaposed qualities of the composition. Once again,
however, he transforms highly abstracted geometric forms
into a kind of tenebristic entity: the way the paint is applied gives the shapes a nervous, vibratory quality. Instead
of a clean, industrial sign of modernity, the elevated becomes a Gothic-like contraption, evoking a sinister air.
Orozco once commented to Alma Reed, "How absurd a
thing is the Elevated . . . It is not quite on the ground and
it is not quite up in the air. And yet it completely spoils
our enjoyment of both."[16] Compared to any precisionist
work of this subject, Orozco's version is a monstrous structure, an absurd thing completely spoiling the environment.

These 1928 New York scenes were among the works
Orozco exhibited at the Downtown Gallery in early 1929.
In the *New York Post*, Margaret Brening was impressed by
how Orozco captured the hectic movement of American
industry.[17] She completely missed his negative commentary on urban life. When some of these same New York
scene paintings were shown at the Delphic Studios in early

1930, Lloyd Goodrich captured the essence of Orozco's meaning:

> His work also shows a new tendency toward abstraction, in which certain motifs appear with a frequency that suggests obsession: in particular the image of shattered fragments of stone and glass— perhaps the unconscious reaction of a life-long revolutionist to our mechanical civilization.[18]

Without a doubt, Orozco's most complete visual statement on the City of New York is the 1931 oil painting *The Dead*, which measures forty-three by thirty-six inches (fig. 13). An urban and allegorical landscape, this composition gives us an aerial view of several skyscrapers falling and being torn apart. This work can be examined in the light of Orozco's recollection of the 1929 crash, written years later in his autobiography:

FIG. 13: *The Dead*, 1931, oil on canvas. Museo de Arte Alvar y Carmen T. de Carrillo Gil.

A morning in 1929, something grave was happening in New York. People were rushing more than was usual. . . . You could hear the sirens of the firemen and the Red Cross sounding furiously. . . . Wall Street and its surrounding area was an infernal sea. Many speculators had thrown themselves from their windows onto the street, their remains picked up by the police. . . . The crash . . . This was the crash, the disaster.[19]

The cause of the disaster is unclear, yet the painting's title gives it symbolic content. The skyscrapers, which signify the prosperity of the 1920s, are falling apart, perhaps reflecting the chaotic situation of the Depression. Orozco was not fond of skyscrapers, even if in his 1929 article in *Creative Art* he recognized them as a new art form. For Orozco, skyscrapers, subways, and other features of the modern metropolis were part of the mechanization process that alienated humans. Perhaps in this painting Orozco gives us all this modernity devouring itself, the bodies of the buildings being torn in half and the broken steel beams and pieces of glass becoming fanglike, sprouting out of jaws. Painted in grays, pinks, and browns, the forms of the skyscrapers are geometric structures turned elastic, serpentlike as they crisscross each other and jump over one another. The aerial viewpoint of the composition reaffirms our sense of looking down into a pit where a struggle for survival is occurring. "The Dead" of the painting's title are not just buildings but possibly also their creators and occupants who have perished in this disaster. One of Orozco's most abstract paintings of the 1930s, *The Dead* is his most searing image of the brutality of modern urban life. It is a picture of apocalyptic convulsion.

Orozco's Notebook 1 (1931) contains over half a dozen pencil sketches of "skeletons" of construction sites around New York City—steel beams, cement blocks, and similar items. Although the sketches seem to have been executed very quickly, there is a constant exploration of diagonals within these construction forms. Undoubtedly, there is a link between a painting like *The Dead* and these sketches,

FIG. 14: *Successful People*, 1931,
oil on canvas. Location unknown.

and it is even possible that these sketches are preliminary ideas for this painting.

Orozco did not find a way to integrate his expressive use of the human figure within his New York scene pictures. One of these attempts, *Successful People* (1931; fig. 14), although a pictorial failure, is still worthy of discussion. An oil on canvas, its location has been unknown since the closing of the Delphic Studios in 1940. We only know *Successful People* by the black-and-white reproduction in Reed's 1932 monograph. It is a vertical composition depicting an old woman in the foreground with her hand to the collar of her dress. Immediately behind her is another figure, whose gender is difficult to discern. This figure wears a bow tie, high collar, and what seems to be a hat. Their necks are stretched tight and their lips are pursed. The eyes of both figures are birdlike; they seem to be squinting, and inside their eyes are pale, small pupils. The old woman's hand is drawn effectively, resembling an arthritic claw. The background is plain and dark, probably thickly painted.

Who are these "successful people"? Obviously, this is Orozco's version of the types he encountered at exhibition openings and cultural cocktail parties. The faces have some of the rigidity and harshness of the face of the schoolteacher in the Anglo-America panel at Dartmouth. The "successful people" are those generous patrons of the arts who know they are above the artist as well as the common people. An American work to compare with this picture would be Grant Wood's *Daughters of Revolution* (Cincinnati Art Museum), painted the following year. The Wood picture is a social lampoon of one of the established institutions of American life, the Daughters of the American Revolution. This work is practically a monochromatic painting in browns, grays, and tans, with very subtle touches of blue. The technique is tight, the expressions on the faces rigid. There is an element of irony present in the Wood painting, a certain cool detachment from the subject. Although we do not know the color structure of Orozco's *Successful People*, the brushwork is agitated and expressive. There is no irony here, but sarcasm. These members of the upper class are indifferent birds of prey, yet birds of prey nevertheless. If the painting does not quite work, it is perhaps due to the artist's caricature-like exaggerations in the drawing of the faces.

We know from Orozco's correspondence with his wife that at certain points during his stay of 1927–32 he considered portrait painting as a possible income-earning genre. With the exception of self-portraits and portraits of contemporary figures whom he either admired (poet and critic Cardoza y Aragón) or despised (the archbishop of Mexico City, Mons. Luis María Martínez), Orozco was not a good portraitist on commission, the way Rivera and Siqueiros could be. Of his New York portraits, only two are known and located. These are *Madame Sikelianos* from 1928 and *Julia Peterkin* from 1930. Both are in the Carillo Gil Museum. These two traditional, academic works are in a visual language that is not typical of Orozco.

Mexican Scenes

Orozco rejected the visual expression of Rivera's *indigenista* stance, not so much the latter's glorification of the pre-Columbian world in his murals, as his folkloric and decorative genre scenes. All of Orozco's correspondence, as well as his autobiography, contain comments against "pretty pictures of Indians." Orozco also rejected the more formal reflection of *indigenismo* in the easel pictures of Charlot and Tamayo and in the prints of Emilio Amero.[20]

Orozco's Mexican scenes are a gallery of images that consciously and critically reject the picturesque reality of the paintings of Rivera and others. Regardless of Orozco's masking of his experience in the Mexican Revolution as "a fun and diverting carnival," that reality as reflected in his paintings, drawings, and prints is anything but carnivalesque.[21]

Soldiers are an important subject in Orozco's Mexican scenes. Rivera could paint them either as romantic heroes or villains, and Siqueiros generally depicted them as a part of the masses on the road to the revolution. In Orozco's hands, soldiers are either brutal destroyers, potential tyrants, or doomed, tragic figures. There is also a racial stereotype at work in Orozco's depictions that critics have generally ignored. His soldiers tend to be the coarsest, most brutal looking Indian types. Rather than stylizing Aztec or Mayan features into beautiful forms, as did Rivera and Montenegro, Orozco painted them as grotesque masks of horrors that instill fear.

Three of Orozco's most powerful and successful easel works dealing with the subject of revolutionary soldiers

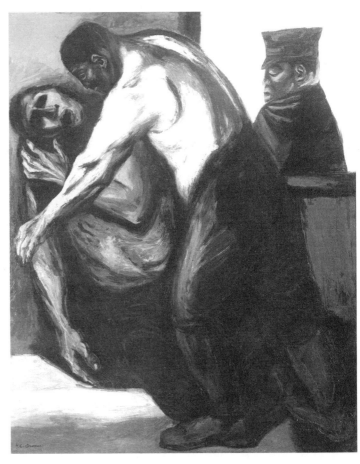

FIG. 15: *Soldado herido*, 1930, oil on canvas. The Cleveland Museum of Art. Gift of Mr. and Mrs. Michael Straight.

were painted in 1930 and 1931. These are *Soldado herido* from 1930 (fig. 15) and *Zapatistas* (fig. 16) and *Barricade* (fig. 17), both from 1931. The first is in the Cleveland Museum of Art, the other two in The Museum of Modern Art in New York City. *Zapatistas* and *Barricade* are also among Orozco's most reproduced works.[22]

Soldado herido shares a similar palette with both *Zapatistas* and *Barricade*, a color structure comprised of browns and grays with areas of intense blues, reds, and yellows. *Soldado herido* depicts an interior scene where one soldier is helping another lie down. They are both shirtless and have obviously removed themselves from an armed conflict outside. On the upper right of the picture, there is a window through which we see a Constitutionalist soldier (forces of Venustiano Carranza and Obregón) with cap and uniform being attentive to a possible battle that we do not see. The sky through the window is thickly painted in a pink-gray color. The interior walls are raw sienna mixed with touches of gray. The floor is yellow ocher. The two soldiers in the interior wear dark blue pants with brown boots. Colors are painted boldly, with strong value contrasts accentuating the dimensionality of the forms. The heads and torsos are drawn powerfully, with the usual emphasis Orozco gives to arms and hands, as well as rib cages. Skin is painted in siennas and ochers, with touches of dark brown. All three figures possess Indian facial features, but unlike other depictions by Orozco, these are not grotesque. The physical movement of the two figures in the interior resembles a deposition scene; a dead or, in this case, dying man is being laid down. Suffering is present; grief is observed.

Zapatistas reflects Orozco's observance of the Zapatista prisoners brought into the Carranza camp:

> I personally did not have a bad time during the revolution, but I saw much brutality, devastation, betrayal. . . . I was with the Carranza forces, and I saw their defeated victims like the poor Zapatista peasants brought in to be executed. There was something suicidal about those Zapatistas, like their leader, they were marked for doom, death. . . . In the end I

FIG. 16: *Zapatistas*, 1931,
oil on canvas, 45 x 55 in.
The Museum of Modern Art,
New York. Anonymous gift.
Photograph © 1996 The Museum
of Modern Art, New York.

FIG. 17: *Barricade*, 1931,
oil on canvas, 55 x 45 in.
The Museum of Modern Art,
New York. Anonymous gift.
Photograph © 1997 The Museum
of Modern Art, New York.

don't trust revolutions or glorify them, since I witnessed too much butchery. Only a fool like Rivera, who was in France during the Mexican revolution can carry on about revolution.[23]

Zapatistas does not exhibit the positive imagery found in works by the likes of Rivera. These peasants are not distributing land or rifles or embracing workers in a show of solidarity. They march forward, bowed figures, followed by shrouded *soldaderas*. The painting is somber, with dark areas of viridian and browns. Red and blue are scattered in the shirts and robes. Four men on horseback loom large over the marching line. Behind them are dark mountains and a stormy sky of dark gray and pale pink. An angular tension is created throughout the whole composition, as the line of figures leans toward the left, while the hills in the background lean toward the right. As in *Soldado herido*, the painting is sober and dramatic. In this picture the viewer associates the red of the clothes with the blood of martyrdom. This painting also reminds one of traditional Christian iconography; the captured Zapatistas are like martyrs being led to their death. They have kept their faith in agrarian revolution and are meeting their end. Orozco writes: "Poor Zapatista peasants, prisoners fallen to the Carrancistas, would be shot in the church atrium."[24]

Zapatistas was one of three works acquired by Stephen C. Clark, a trustee of The Museum of Modern Art. When Clark visited Orozco, he praised his talents, telling him he was one of the most significant artists of the period. Clark also suggested that Orozco paint larger easel pictures. He indicated that he would buy several of them at $2,500 a piece for his private collection and eventually donate them to The Museum of Modern Art.[25] In 1931, Clark purchased three Orozco paintings—*Zapatistas*, *Barricade*, and *El cementerio*—for $7,500, and in 1937 all three were given anonymously to The Museum of Modern Art.[26]

Barricade is a slightly different second version of Orozco's 1926 fresco mural *La trinchera* at the National Preparatory School. The fresco is practically monochrome, executed in tans, black, brown, and white against a blood-red sky.

La trinchera is an image of agonizing defeat. The composition contains a bare-chested man placed diagonally across the center. To the left, another man with two cartridge belts across his torso bends in the same direction. The back of this figure is to the viewer. These two figures together give the impression of a single crucified figure. *Barricade* has more color than the fresco; the browns and tans are complemented by various blues, deep purples, and red. Being an oil on canvas, the figures are thickly painted, while some of the background areas are flat. The men's hands, feet, and torsos are drawn in an exaggerated realism, with particular emphasis on the joints and fingers. Again, the two principal figures are juxtaposed front and back, giving as a unit the impression of a distorted crucifixion. While in the fresco a kneeling soldier grieves on the lower right, in the oil painting Orozco replaces this one figure with three. These are all in profile and stacked one upon another. In the distant background, a head in profile seems to be screaming. This 1931 easel painting depicts the figures still engaged in battle, while the 1926 mural panel is definitely a scene of defeat.

Noting the constant explorations of diagonals in these easel pictures, it is important to look into the artist's sketchbooks at this time. Notebook 1 (1931) contains over forty highly schematic and geometric sketches that explore variations and diagonals. Next to these, Orozco writes:

Without diagonals there is no geometry, pure mechanics.

Diagonals are a *geometric after taste.*

Study of energy: nature itself, the works of art and the *machines,* that which is mechanic.[27]

Elsewhere in the same sketchbook, he notes:

In a painting, the *articulations* or points of anchor are found in the *intersection* of diagonals, in the *axles* or *sides of the painting.* The *forces* are applied in any point of the aforementioned lines.[28]

The sketches and notes are signs that Orozco was seriously studying the process of picture-making. Although these sketches are crude and minimal, they are experiments that are eventually absorbed and synthesized into the easel pictures.

Toward the end of Notebook 1, he writes regarding composition:

> A sculpture, a painting, an architecture is a space divided in unequal parts organized in a *system*. Each part is also a space divided in unequal parts organized in a system. The organization of the parts is established by means of relationships *determined* by reason. The relationships are of: proportion, form, color, tone, density, position, character, meaning. The most important relationships in the totality establishes most powerfully the *unity* of the composition.[29]

Clearly, the pictorial dynamism of certain of Orozco's easel pictures, such as *Soldado herido*, *Zapatistas*, and *Barricade*, have their gestation, however abstractly and conceptual, in the jottings of the two notebooks of 1931–32.

The Mexican Revolution created its own particular iconography. Where there had been Catholic saints since the time of the conquest, now there were secular revolutionary leaders like Villa and Zapata. After the deaths of Zapata in 1919 and Villa in 1923 and during the 1930s, their figures became mythologized in historical accounts, novels, paintings, and eventually films. As a caricaturist for the anarcho-syndicalist periodical *La Vanguardia* in 1915 (which was allied with the forces of Carranza and Obregón), Orozco created satirical drawings of the so-called peasant rebels, Villa and Zapata. For *La Vanguardia*, these men and their followers were seen as agrarian, backward, and religious. The anarcho-syndicalists of *La Vanguardia* sided with the Constitutionalists, whose roots were urban and secular and who favored scientific progress.[30]

Over time, Orozco's view of Zapata would change and emerge in a 1930 easel work executed in California, as well as in the Dartmouth mural. Zapata evolved in Orozco's hand from a bloody and obscurantist peasant to a noble martyr. Perhaps this change was due to the artist's realization of Zapata's link to anarchism and antifederalism, as well as the respect for Zapata of the imprisoned (in the United States) anarcho-communist Ricardo Flores Magón, whom Orozco admired. Orozco did not change his perception of Villa. *Pancho Villa* (1931; fig. 18) is a small painting wherein Orozco depicts Villa as a powerful and ruthless figure.

Francisco Villa was born Doroteo Arango Arámbula in San Juan del Rio, Province of Durango, in 1878. When he was sixteen years old, he murdered a local man and fled his region. In time, he assumed the name of Francisco Villa. He was first an outlaw and, as one, developed his own tactics of guerrilla warfare. These he utilized years later when he joined the revolution. In 1910, he took part in the peasant uprisings in the North against the regime of Porfirio Díaz. He was allied for a time with Carranza, Obregón, and Zapata, but by 1915 he had broken with the first two. Due to the United States government's recognition of a Carranza presidency, Villa started to attack border towns in the United States. President Woodrow Wilson sent General John Pershing and his troops to push Villa back into Mexico. By late 1921, Villa "retired" to Canutillo in the North, where he ran a small shop that produced iron beams. According to historian Enrique Krauze, on July 20, 1923, Villa was assassinated by Jesús Salas Barraza and others, allegedly on the orders of General Obregón.[31]

FIG. 18: *Pancho Villa*, 1931, oil on canvas. Museo de Arte Alvar y Carmen T. de Carrillo Gil.

Orozco painted Villa dressed in a white cotton shirt and trousers, typical of peasants from the South, where Zapata, not Villa, was from. He holds a gun in one hand, while with the other he pulls the hair of a naked, pregnant woman. At his feet lies a nude male figure who is about to be killed, if he is not dead already. Behind Villa is a tumultuous mixture of his followers and crouching figures who seem to be begging for mercy. In the background, there is also a house on fire. Villa's face is fierce, with dark eyes and clenched teeth. The overall coloristic structure is one of browns, tans, and grays, with scattered patches of pale blue. The paint is applied sparingly, almost simulating a dry brush technique and allowing the grain of the canvas to show through. The overall drawing is minimal and sparse. At times, Orozco's background as a political cartoonist is evident in certain exaggerations in the figures. Orozco interprets Villa as a violent bandit, not as a revolutionary leader.

FIG. 19: *Zapata Entering a Peasant's Hut*, 1930, oil on canvas, 178.4 x 122.6 cm. The Art Institute of Chicago. Gift of Joseph Winterbotham Collection, 1941.35. Photograph © 1999 The Art Institute of Chicago. All rights reserved.

When Orozco depicted Zapata in 1930, it was from a tragic or doomed point of view. His *Zapata Entering a Peasant's Hut* (fig. 19), executed in San Francisco shortly after he completed the mural at Pomona College in Claremont, is dark and claustrophobic. Painted in dark reds, browns, and blacks with touches of pale gray and blue, the composition consists of Zapata dominating the upper center of the picture plane. The hut he enters is dark. Two soldiers with their backs turned to the viewer are on Zapata's left, while two grieving figures kneel in the foreground. Zapata's face is tragic and masklike, resembling the dramatic pre-Columbian forms of Olmec and Toltec sculptures. The narrative within the painting is unclear. Yet we discern a desperate situation without solution. The despair is accentuated by the grieving figures, which again are reminiscent of the Christian iconography of the lamentation. If Orozco's *Pancho Villa* represents the revolutionary as macho bandit leaving chaos in his wake, his *Zapata Entering a Peasant's Hut* is the revolutionary on his way to inevitable martyrdom.[32]

What is interesting in Orozco's, Rivera's, and Siqueiros's

depictions of Zapata is that they agree on the ideological and personal superiority of the leader of the South over the banditry of Villa—thus their positive contributions to Zapatista iconography. Orozco, due to his anti-agrarian political background, was the last of the three muralists to accept this view. Both Rivera and Siqueiros, but particularly Rivera, saw Zapata and portrayed him as an important element in the process of popular self-empowerment of the Mexican people. Orozco's representation of Zapata is one filtered through a pessimistic view of history—perhaps one based on the belief of populism's eventual defeatism.

Rivera, Charlot, and lesser artists painted Mexican scenes from at least two perspectives. Scenes of optimism regarding the revolution, based on either a Marxist or liberal perspective, was one. The other was genre scenes that celebrated folk culture and matriarchy in particular. These last, at their worst, could be exotic views that simplified a more complicated reality. In part because of his disenchantment with the revolution, with the betrayal of the anarcho-syndicalist movement by the government, and in light of his own antipathy to any *indigenista* stance, Orozco chose to depict Mexican scenes in a critical, if sometimes overly gloomy, light.

Orozco was most prolific as an easel painter when he was not involved with a major mural project. Easel paintings were executed before and after the *Prometheus* mural; the same holds true when he was working at the New School for Social Research and at Dartmouth.

In his easel pictures, Orozco depicted the darker side of reality, be this through New York scenes or Mexican subjects. His metropolis is not the same as the precisionists'; the New York pictures are about alienation and destruction. These are negative images of urban life. His Mexico is not Rivera's or Siqueiros's; his paintings contain tragic views of the revolution and the devastation it left in its wake. In one of his sketchbooks, Orozco defined expressionism, a style that suits his work:

Static subjects. Many religious themes. Suppress the object. Exciting. Extravagant. Dynamic. Loud. Summary. First planes. Moves forward. Great forms.

Monumental. Warm. Thick chromatic substance. Rough: scratches. Like rock that has not been carved. Allows one to see the work, the hand, the craft. Expressive deformation of the objects. Supremacy of the diagonal, acute angle, in opposition to the borders of the painting. Primal.[33]

With these words, Orozco could have easily been describing his own art: views of New York that captured the brutality of the city; Mexican subjects that turned "Indians with flowers" on their head and evoked the tragedy of religious art through the revolution.

Drawings and Lithographs

Rivera, Siqueiros, and Orozco all drew extensively. Drawing was not just the first step in the process of designing the composition of murals, it was also a medium in its own right, where works could be created independently of easel and mural painting. In Rivera's drawings both the rigor and boredom of academicism is present. Siqueiros could be a powerful draftsman, particularly during the late 1920s and into the 1930s, yet at his worst his drawings are exaggerated and overly mannered. On the other hand, Orozco's weak drawings are no more than caricatures with monumental aspirations. At the same time, his background as a caricaturist also gives his drawings a more experimental and audacious slant. In terms of content, Orozco's graphic work is both more satirical and dramatic than Rivera's and Siqueiros's.

Orozco discovered the medium of lithography during his second stay in the United States. He used the lithographic technique in its own right, exploring subjects not found in his drawings and paintings. Like Rivera and Siqueiros, Orozco also used lithography to recycle and popularize earlier images from murals. With few exceptions, these tend to be his weakest prints. Like all traditionally trained artists, Orozco believed drawing to be the basis of all art; he declared this belief verbally on various occasions throughout his life. More than that, he explored it throughout his life-long, intense involvement with graphic work. This is evident from the *México en revolución* series of the late 1920s through the allegorical ink drawings of the late 1940s.

Drawings

Orozco's first one-person exhibition in New York City consisted of his *México en revolución* series of forty-three ink drawings.[34] It is possible that Orozco had completed twenty to twenty-two of these drawings by early 1927. He sent these ahead to the United States with Anita Brenner, since he feared a repetition of his earlier experience with United States Customs.[35] The rest of the series was completed in New York City during 1928, though perhaps the last six drawings were finished in early 1929.[36] In her 1932 monograph, Alma Reed reproduced all forty-three drawings under the heading "'Mexico in Revolution' Drawings and Lithographs from Sketches Made between 1913 and 1917."[37] There were no lithographs in this series; all were ink and wash drawings on paper, each measuring approximately twenty-four by thirty-six inches. Reed created the legend that these drawings were based on sketches made between 1913 and 1917. It seems unlikely that Orozco kept sketchbooks while he worked at *La Vanguardia* as a political caricaturist in 1915, as well as later when he drew for other newspapers. No sketchbooks from this period have been located. Without a doubt, Orozco saw in real life some of the episodes that he transformed into images in the *México en revolución* series. Yet by the time he sat down to draw these in the late 1920s, over a decade had passed since he had witnessed some of these scenes. Distance helped him fictionalize, choose a point of view, and go beyond mere reporting. Other compositions in the series are purely imaginative. They are filled with the misogyny of the symbolism of Julio Ruelas, an important influence on Orozco's early aesthetic development.

Five works from this series will be discussed here. These are from the group executed in New York City, and they represent traditional themes for the artist: anticlericalism, disasters, corruption, and devastation. All of these drawings were made with both pen and brush, possibly over a

FIG. 20: *Evicción*, 1928, ink on paper. Private collection.

light pencil sketch delineating the overall composition. The washes range from very light gray, allowing the white of the paper to show through, to deep blacks. Since Orozco did not use the very best ink, but instead worked with what was available to him, the drawings have faded to a range of black-browns; some of the grays over time have become sepia.

Evicción (fig. 20) depicts a group of five revolutionaries—three in the foreground, two in the background—evicting five priests and one *sacristan* (adult altar server). The revolutionaries have been drawn with a great economy of means; a few strokes of the pen produced their broad hats. Clad in white, these figures have cartridge belts strapped across their torsos. They are not drawn as individuals but as symbols of the revolution. The priests, who are being pushed out of the picture plane to the left, do possess individual features: they are all grotesque. Orozco washed them in as a large black mass comprised of six bodies. Their coloration makes them resemble a group of shrieking vultures. As late as the 1940s, when he executed the portrait of Mons. Luis María Martínez, the archbishop of Mexico City, Orozco referred to him as the "Big Vulture." In his autobiography, he recalled the evictions of churches:

The church of El Carmen was also assaulted and given to the workers. . . . Saints, confession boxes and altars were chopped for firewood for cooking by the women, we took the ornaments of the priests and altars. We all came out decorated with rosaries, medals and scapulars.[38]

In this drawing, Orozco's usual anticlericalism is present. He does not, however, glorify the revolutionaries. They are simply abstracted. Orozco is better at attacking than affirming, and the bloated priests are a perfect target. Allies of the established order, the clergy depicted here are not defenders of the peasantry but rather exploiters who tell the masses that justice is to be found only in heaven.

Tren dinamitado (fig. 21) prefigures the apocalyptic qualities of the 1934 mural *Catarsis*. The composition intermingles the industrial forms of a blown-up train with female nudes. Between the slopes of two hills is a background littered with wheels and fragments of various wagons. In the central background, between the intersection of two converging diagonals, there is a blasted wooden structure, possibly an electric pole. Lying across the foreground are three dead female nudes. One has her head covered by a piece of metal; blood drips down an arm, breast, and leg. The other two nudes are drawn in a foreshortened manner; one has her head toward the viewer, the other her feet. The nude whose head is visible has both arms tied together. Who are these women? Hostages raped

FIG. 21: *Tren dinamitado*, 1928, ink on paper, 12 ¼ x 19 in. The Philadelphia Museum of Art. Purchased: Lola Downin Peck Fund from the estate of Carl Zigrosser.

by their captors? Depicted in positions of submission, they become another expression of the artist's misogyny. Once again, Orozco's women are deprived of a life-affirming identity. They are either schoolgirls who will be corrupted, whores, or victims of absurd brutality. Rivera, on the other hand, opted to empathize and glorify Mexican matriarchs in his paintings and drawings, particularly those of the most humble classes. He also depicted women as revolutionaries in the Ministry of Public Education murals.

Blown-up trains were a very common occurrence throughout the Mexican Revolution. First literature and later films were filled with this imagery, generally depicted

FIG. 22: *La boda del general*, 1928, ink on paper. Private collection.

as exciting opportunities for battle and for encountering the enemy unexpectedly. This is not the case in this drawing. *Tren dinamitado* presents an image of chaotic, absurd death, made stark by the white nude bodies in the foreground. In this work, Orozco pulls the rug of romanticism from under the revolution. Here is death and destruction, meaningless as ever.

One of the most grotesque drawings from this series is *La boda del general* (fig. 22). The composition depicts a minimally rendered street where the dark walls of two buildings are visible on the left side and in the background. In the center, slightly to the right, stand four figures. Two are common revolutionary soldiers standing in the middle ground. One is barefoot, the other has his back to the viewer. They are drawn in an almost shorthand style, a few lines and bold washes of gray and black. The figure facing us is blunt, the features of his face grotesque. These features are evidence of "mestizaje"—the racial by-product of Indian and Spanish. Yet Orozco always makes the features more Indian than Spanish, again a clue to his own anti-*indigenista* position. Unlike Rivera and even Siqueiros, Orozco associates the Indian not with a glorious pre-Cortesian past but rather with brutality, coarseness, and ignorance. This reflects a patronizing attitude similar to the position of thinkers like Vasconcelos, who believed in the "civilizing" presence of Spain over the native cultures of the Americas.

The two central figures in this work are the general himself and the young wife he has just taken. The general wears a wide-brimmed hat with the seal of the Mexican flag on its center. His face, although more detailed, is similar to those of the soldiers in the background. It is a grotesque mask covered with a wild mustache. His left leg has a wooden peg below the knee. His pawlike hands clutch the voluptuous female figure. She covers her face with her hands; this is not the fate she would have wished for herself. Is she perhaps marrying the general to save her family or her family's property, or is she a human spoil of war? The drawing is an image of corruption and abuse of power. The new revolutionary caudillos, like the ones of the previous regime, take what they want, when they want it. Orozco evoked in his recollection of the revolution this state of corruption and chaos:

FIG. 23: *Los heridos*, 1928, ink on paper. Museo de Arte Alvar y Carmen T. de Carrillo Gil.

Song, drama and barbarism. Buffoons and dwarfs following hangmen in cahoots with smiling procuresses. Insolent commandants burning with alcohol, demanding everything with gun in hand. Shots in dark streets, at night, followed by screams, blasphemies, and unforgivable insults. Broken storefronts, dry blows, pain, more bullets.[39]

Lastly, the drawings *Los heridos* (fig. 23) and *El fusilado* (fig. 24) form a telling pair of the remnants of revolution and war. *Los heridos* (the wounded) is very similar in content and graphic technique to works of the 1920s by the Germans Max Beckmann, George Grosz, and Otto Dix.

The Germans were depicting the remains of World War I: people with amputated limbs and all sorts of disabilities, the corrupt, and the deranged. Orozco in *Los heridos* also depicts the remains of a conflict, in this case, the Mexican Revolution.

Los heridos portrays a makeshift hospital ward in what could be a barn. The battlefield is obviously not far away. In the background are women mourning the dead or caring for the wounded. Two soldiers enter the ward bearing a stretcher with a sheet-covered corpse. A few typical figures with serapes and broad-brimmed hats stand about. The ground is littered with bodies, some under sheets, some not. In the foreground of the drawing to the left, two figures (they could be doctors, nurses, or orderlies) struggle over a dying patient whose head, arm, and legs are visible below them. To their right are the real horrors: two men with amputated limbs, one sideways, the other turning his back to the viewer. The first has part of his left leg missing and a bandage from the crotch to the stump at the knee. Both arms are also missing from below the elbows. The face is bandaged from the top of the upper lip to the cropped mane of hair. The mouth is semiopen, showing some teeth, perhaps expressing pain. The other figure has also lost part of both legs, as well as the right arm from below the elbow; above the elbow there is a bandage. These mutilated torsos are drawn with great strength, demonstrating Orozco's knowledge of the structure of the human body. The floor of this makeshift hospital seems to be plain dirt upon which a drama is played out; namely, the agony of the dying and mutilated and the fatalistic indifference of the attendants, evident in the figures in the background.

El fusilado, the executed one, is one of Orozco's most powerful drawings in his entire production as a draftsman. A composition of tense angles, it renders the figures against the architecture and the architecture against the ground. This work contains nine figures spaced throughout the foreground, middle ground, and background. Tonally, the drawing ranges from the deep blacks of the immediate foreground (the shawls of the women and entranceways to the building) to the white of the paper showing through a pale gray wash, which becomes the sky. The scene portrays the activities in front of a building that could be the headquarters of a revolutionary chief. A *fusilado*—someone who has just been executed by a firing squad—is carried on a stretcher toward the left and into the background. One arm falls outside the stretcher, while the dead man's hat lies on his stomach. This figure is drawn opaquely, with a great deal of black ink. The stretcher is carried by two men wearing hats. In front of them, two soldiers with rifles march. These four figures were sketched in with light

pencil and ink. All are covered with a moderate gray wash. In the foreground, drawn forcefully and darkly with a brush, is a hatless old man, a woman, and a small girl. Both of the females are covered with shawls. Their backs turned to the viewer, they follow the corpse of the fusilado. Nearby, a figure in a serape and hat walks to the right holding a rifle. We barely see his face, since most of it is covered by the serape. Might he have been one of the executioners?

FIG. 24: *El fusilado*, 1928, ink on paper. Private collection.

Every element in this drawing works; there is a balance between the quick sketch and the carefully modeled forms. The synthesis of understated, violent content and the formal structure of angles and rectangles creates an image with impact reminiscent of Goya and Daumier, artists known and admired by Orozco. Psychologically, *El fusilado* evokes both grief and despair. The executed are buried by their families. The executioners follow their orders. Against the tomblike building in the background, the figures seem small and insignificant, resigned to their daily tasks. This work is one of many footnotes to the revolution, to any revolution. The vanquished are further victimized by the victors. Men are executed by firing squads, their families left behind in

ruin. They are not entitled to a new social order.

Orozco's series of drawings *México en revolución* can rightly be compared to Goya's *Desastres de la guerra* prints, both in its narrative, episodic quality and bleak view of armed conflict and its aftermath. In his correspondence with his wife, Orozco always referred to these drawings as *"los horrores"* (the horrors). Orozco, like Goya, can be both somber and satirical. The literary equivalent to these drawings is the novel *Los de abajo* (*The Underdogs*) by Orozco's compatriot Mariano Azuela.

Trained as a physician, Azuela (1873–1952) was a liberal supporter of Francisco I. Madero. After the collapse of the Díaz regime, Azuela was made director of education of the State of Jalisco. He joined Villa's army in the North as a doctor after General Victoriano Huerta assassinated President Madero. Azuela's knowledge of the revolution was acquired firsthand, as he was active in Villa's army from 1912 to 1915. By the end of 1915, he was in exile in El Paso, Texas, where he published *Los de abajo* in serial form. The definitive edition of the novel was printed in Mexico City in 1920.[40] Credited with being the first realistic depiction of the Mexican Revolution, *Los de abajo* narrates in episodic form the story of Demetrio Macías, an Indian forced to side with the rebels to save his family. In the course of battle he becomes both a compulsive and corrupt militarist, eventually rising to the rank of general in Villa's army. The background of the entire novel is filled with battle scenes, executions, and lootings. The characters range from loyal peasants who want land and freedom to turncoats and women of easy virtue. Defeated and disillusioned by the end of the novel, Macías is ambushed and killed by former allies. Filled with bitter irony, the novel lays out the brutal excesses of the revolution and the betrayal of its idealistic principles by the new power structure. The book does in words what Orozco's drawings do in images.

It is no accident that Orozco was approached in early 1929 to illustrate an English translation of the book. He informed Charlot:

FIG. 26: Illustration for *The Underdogs*, 1929, ink on paper. Location unknown.

FIG. 25: Illustration for *The Underdogs*, 1929, ink on paper. Location unknown. (facing page)

Enrique Murguía was here, he is a lawyer at the Mexican embassy, if you do not know him I will send you a letter of introduction, he comes from Mexico, is friendly, young, a drinker, ex-admirer of Diego and the translator into english of Azuela's *The Underdogs*.

Diego will do the illustrations and I the front and back covers, it will be published by Brentano.[41]

When Azuela's *The Underdogs* was published in 1929, it contained a reproduction of a painting by Rivera on the cover (*The Burning of Judas Figures*, a 1923 fresco at the Ministry of Public Education in Mexico City) and several brush and ink illustrations by Orozco.[42] Orozco produced five vignettes that were used as chapter headings and five full-page illustrations. Of these last, two go beyond mere illustrations and stand as powerful drawings in their own right (figs. 25 and 26). One depicts a highly abstracted battle scene, where masses of figures descend upon one another at different angles. In the background, both a blasted tree and a stormy sky can be seen, the latter evoked by a brushed black stain. Throughout the drawing—using a series of rough, spiky lines—Orozco creates the illusion of heaps of figures being crushed and stabbed. The angular tensions and scumbled lines of this drawing create a surface similar to that of a Jackson Pollock drip painting from the 1940s.

The other illustration is a cleaner and more monumental drawing that depicts a revolutionary soldier wearing a broad hat, a rifle leaning against his arm. In his hand he holds a glass (of alcohol no doubt). With the other arm, he holds a woman with braided hair who is sitting on his lap, her back to the viewer. The squinting eye and twisted mouth on the soldier's face denote intoxication. The entire drawing has been executed with a brush. Some lines are thin, but most tend to be wide and rough. Both figures are drawn as solid, powerful masses. Yet again individual identity is either generalized or missing, transforming the figures into symbols for every soldier and *soldadera*, a term used to define common-law wives of soldiers during the revolution.

FIG. 27: *New York Subway*, 1929,
charcoal on paper.
Location unknown.

FIG. 28: *The Committee on Art*, 1932,
ink on paper. Location unknown.

The last two drawings I discuss reflect more directly the environment of New York City. These are *New York Subway* from 1929 (fig. 27), a charcoal drawing, and *The Committee on Art* from 1932 (fig. 28), an ink on paper.

The charcoal, whose location is unknown, could be the companion piece to the oil painting *The Subway*. The composition renders a platform that ends in a black square in the background. The beams on the ceiling as well as the columns are drawn as the solid pieces of steel that they are. Orozco, however, gives these forms gritty, coarse surfaces, evoking dirt. Four figures are visible—these are nothing more than black silhouettes of automatons. The work again is the antithesis of the dynamic, lively depictions of the same subject by the artists of the Fourteenth Street School. Orozco's subway platform is a steel and concrete underground where no exit is visible. In his eyes it becomes a claustrophobic tomb or mine shaft rather than a waiting station for the latest form of modern transportation.

The Committee on Art is another of the artist's visual comments on the rich and powerful art patrons he encountered at art exhibition openings. Orozco's background as a political caricaturist comes across not only in his ability to have the lines do his bidding with great economy of means but also in the grotesquely drawn faces of the personages.

This drawing contains eleven figures proceeding friezelike to the left. Seven male figures form the background. These are drawn simply with square-jawed heads (some with hair, some without), two wearing glasses. Their bodies are all similar: massive and with boxy overcoats with two feet at the bottom. The faces are all expressionless. The male at the end of the line, although balding, has an uncanny resemblance to Alfred H. Barr Jr., the founding director of The Museum of Modern Art. In the foreground, three immense women wearing fur coats are followed by a young man with puckered lips. These figures are drawn in vitriol, not ink: the women are bloated, their faces mean and aggressive, like birds of prey. Two of them wear what seem to be top hats. They walk with authority. The figure at the head of the line holds a cane. The young man follows the three women with a blank stare, like the other males depicted in the drawing. Could these women be powerful museum trustees? Whoever they are, it is clear that they are the makers of taste, the elite. To Orozco, they could be the admirers of Rivera and French modernism.

This drawing has much in common, both in satirical content and technical execution, with the drawings and watercolors Grosz produced after his exile to New York. Grosz's drawings, like Orozco's, are vicious commentaries on the superfluous lives of the lovers of culture. These two artists have a deeper bond that informs their critical visions; both were outsiders within American culture, as well as, by 1932, former leftists. They lived through revolutions, the Depression, and, in Grosz's case, even fascism, and survived as pessimists. Satire, as evident in *The Committee on Art* as well as in other works, made the dreadful present easier to bear.

Orozco used the medium of drawing in different ways. It served as the quick notation for more ambitious work in another medium and as a technique in its own right, such as the series *México en revolución*.

Lithographs

Orozco started working in the lithographic medium after his arrival in New York City. The new technique of lithography represented for Orozco an opportunity to satisfy his natural inclination for experimentation. This medium offered the possibility of producing many copies of an image, which could be sold to a larger market for an accessible price. Orozco's letters to both his wife and Charlot during this time (1928–29) are filled with comments regarding the salability of prints.

Orozco began his first lithography in early February 1928, as he explained in a letter to Charlot:

LITHOGRAPHY: I am going to make some, it is easy, not necessary to do it in stone, there are some special plates, I already have two of these. There is a man here, a Mr. Miller, who has a lithography shop and makes the impressions for the art galleries. The plates that I bought (26 x 43 cm) cost 50

FIG. 29: *Vaudeville in Harlem*, 1928,
lithograph. Private collection.

cents, the impression of the first 12 proofs costs
10 dollars and each one after that is 25 cents, plus
the paper. It is expensive for me, but I will see how
I can pay.

There are many possibilities for any kind of
engraving. In linoleum it is very easy.[43]

Between 1928 and 1930, Orozco executed nineteen
lithographs, seventeen of which were printed by George
Miller in his shop on Fourteenth Street.[44] Two of Orozco's
last lithographs of 1930, *Cabeza de campesina* and *Tres
generaciones*, were printed from zinc plates by Will Barnet
at the Art Students League lithography shop.[45] Orozco's
most prolific year with the lithographic medium was 1930,
when he executed ten of the nineteen prints he produced while in New York. These were most probably
pulled before he went to Claremont, California, to paint
the *Prometheus* fresco at Pomona College, or later while
back in New York preparing to paint the New School murals. As with easel paintings and drawings, Orozco did not
produce lithographs while working on a mural project.

Among the prints done in New York, *Manos*, *Aflicción*,
Franciscano, *Embarazada*, *Cabeza de campesina*, and *Tres
generaciones* are lithographic versions of various details
from the Preparatoria murals. These murals were known by

a larger public in the United States, due in part to the publication in various art magazines of the photographs taken by Tina Modotti and others. Therefore, Orozco probably recycled these themes in the medium of lithography in the hopes that their previous recognizability would aid in their sale.

Six pencil and ink studies exist for six of the images Orozco executed in lithography. These are *Vaudeville in Harlem, Requiem, Retaguardia, Soldados Mexicanos, Revolución,* and *Manos entrelazadas.* The simple, linear studies lay out the overall elements of the composition. In scale they are slightly smaller than the prints that are based on them. Apart from these studies, Orozco seems to have drawn directly on the plate with the lithographic crayon or ink, without much preparation.[46]

Orozco sold his lithographs through the Weyhe Gallery. It is possible that Carl Zigrosser (1891–1975), an art dealer who ran the Weyhe Gallery in the 1920s and 1930s and became the curator of prints and drawings at the Philadelphia Museum of Art (1940–63), made the initial contact with Orozco. They did, after all, share a common political background in anarchism. After the Delphic Studios opened in 1929, Orozco sold his lithographs there and at Weyhe. Generally, his editions were a maximum of a hundred copies, although the smaller editions consisted of twenty-two copies; in some cases, like *Vaudeville in Harlem* and *Manos entrelazadas,* there is no information on the number of copies. A problem with Orozco's United States lithographs is the different titles given a single work by either the artist or Alma Reed. A work like *Negros ahorcados* is known by at least three different titles: *The Hanged Men, Negroes,* and the second most used title, *The American Scene.*

Vaudeville in Harlem (fig. 29) was Orozco's first lithograph. Executed in early February 1928, the work depicts

FIG. 30: *Requiem,* 1928, lithograph. Private collection.

FIG. 31: *Franciscano*, 1930,
lithograph. Private collection.

the audience blocklike and silhouetted in the dark; four
figures involved in some sort of acrobatic act occupy the
light-filled stage. There is no specific indication that this is
a Harlem scene; only the title of the work tells us so. The
work juxtaposes the liveliness of the performers with the
denser forms of the audience. In his autobiography as well
as in letters to both Charlot and Margarita, Orozco ex-
presses his fascination with Harlem's nightlife. He visited
clubs and theaters there with regularity, at one point in
the company of García Lorca. This print is a remembrance
of that life, as well as a homage to the popular theater, an
art form that always interested Orozco. The entire work is
drawn with lithographic crayon, without the use of ink.
The subject of the theater or vaudeville can be found in
the drawings and watercolors of Daumier, an artist much
admired by Orozco, and also in the work of artists whose
work Orozco encountered while in New York City, such as

John Sloan and other Ashcan School painters. Ultimately, for Orozco, this subject has to do with modern city life, a public yet strange place where people sit in darkness and escape through the action on the lighted stage.

Requiem (fig. 30), also from 1928, is one of Orozco's most powerful prints. According to the artist's correspondence with his wife, the work sold out at the Weyhe Gallery quickly, and the *New York Evening Post* (December 15, 1928) cited it as one of the best prints of the year. It was also selected by the American Institute of Graphic Arts as one of the fifty best prints of 1928.

The composition has much in common with previous easel works by the artist, such as *El muerto*. The work renders a mourning scene in which five figures surround the front door of a house wherein a wake takes place. Of the five figures, three are standing, one kneels with her back to the viewer, while the other, prostrate and weeping, covers her face with her hands. Two of the figures are male, the rest female. They are all dressed humbly, in typical Indian garb: barefoot, serapes, shawls. Two lighted candlesticks are held by two of the figures. Throughout the print, the blacks are deep and dark, the grays coarsely applied. The bodies are modeled simply yet solidly. Even though this is an outdoor scene at night, there is a claustrophobic air throughout the work. Grief is a heaviness that cannot be shaken. Francisco Goitia's easel painting *Tata Jesucristo*, another wake scene, comes to mind—in both works mourning is represented as infinite and deep. It has become a way of life.

Franciscano (1930; fig. 31) is the best of the prints based on details from the Preparatoria murals. This lithograph has also been given the titles of *El fraile y el indio* and *The Franciscan and the Indian*. The work portrays a friar arched over an emaciated Indian, whom he is embracing and kissing. Although only 12 $^3/_8$ by 10 $^1/_2$ inches, the print possesses the same somber grandeur as the original fresco. Both figures are monumental, drawn solidly and with exaggeration. This is not the usual anticlerical Orozco. The print, like the mural, transcends simple anticlericalism to make an ambiguous statement regarding human solidarity. This friar could be the soul mate to other larger-than-life figures Orozco has depicted—Prometheus, Christ, and Zapata—figures who in the eyes of the artist sacrifice themselves for those on the margins of society. Orozco transforms this composition into an icon of compassion. At the same time, the friar seems to be overwhelming the Indian, as if choking him. Is this perhaps an image of oppression?

Negros ahorcados, also from 1930 (fig. 32), is the last of Orozco's lithographs printed in New York City. Interestingly, Orozco's first and last lithographs executed in the United States are the only ones with American themes, and both, one indirectly and the other directly, make reference to African American subjects. In the New School murals, Orozco painted an African and an African American with a great deal of dignity and sympathy. The artist was aware of the conditions of social injustice that African Americans experienced. The theme of lynching is a common one in American art of the 1930s. Both George Biddle and Thomas Hart Benton, friends of Orozco, dealt with the subject of lynching directly and indirectly in their work of the 1930s.[47]

Orozco's *Negros ahorcados* was included by Alma Reed in two exhibitions in the 1930s dealing with lynching, "An Art Commentary on Lynching" held in the winter of 1935 at the New York Arthur V. Newton Galleries and sponsored by the N.A.A.C.P., and the 1935 antilynching exhibition sponsored by the John Reed Club and held at the A.C.A. Gallery.[48] The 1970 Luigi Marrozzini and Clemente Orozco V. catalog erroneously states that *Negros ahorcados* was specially executed by Orozco as a fund-raising contribution to the American Civil Rights Congress. This is not possible, since this organization did not come into being until June 1946.[49]

Another reason for Orozco's selection of this subject, beyond his personal solidarity with African Americans, may be found in Alma Reed's politics. As a former journalist with liberal tendencies, Reed was surely aware of the epidemic of lynchings in the United States throughout the 1920s and 1930s, and she could have even suggested the topic to Orozco. The print is based on a photograph reproduced in the *Labor Defender* showing the burned and contorted figure of George Hughes, lynched by a mob in Sherman, Texas.[50]

Negros ahorcados is one of the artist's most horrific

prints. The work portrays two thick tree trunks from which hang the nude bodies of four lynched black men. Flames rising from the lower right of the lithograph are starting to consume the bodies. Three of the bodies have been drawn in the background as little more than silhouettes. In the foreground, off-center and in detail, is the principal fig-

ure. This figure has a frozen expression of terror on his face; his eyes and mouth are wide open. His left hand has been severed and his genitalia mutilated. The figures, as well as the tree trunks, have been drawn with the lithographic crayon in wide, agitated strokes. The flames have been drawn by scratching off the lithographic crayon surface. This graphic work is the most expressionistic of all Orozco's early prints, to be rivaled only by his last aquatints of 1944.[51]

In the April 1934 issue of the *Print Collectors Quarterly*, Laurence Schmeckebier published a laudatory article on Orozco's prints. The author considered the prints important not only for their dramatic subjects and straightforward technique but above all for the "torn and jagged outlines" of their power-

FIG. 32: *Negros ahorcados*, 1930, lithograph. Private collection.

ful, overall design. The article was illustrated with the prints *Retaguardia*, *Requiem*, *Bandera*, *Pueblo Mexicano*, and *Paisaje Mexicano*. Schmeckebier concluded the article by stating: "The monumental character of Orozco's work lies in the weight of his simple elementary masses combined with the dramatic intensity with which these masses are manipulated."[52] Just four years after Orozco had completed his last lithograph in the United States, he was gaining international attention (the *Quarterly* was published in London) for work in a medium he had started working with only seven years earlier.

Orozco's work in the printmaking mediums has been studied by J. H. Hopkins and Luigi Marrozzini.[53] Hopkins's book lacks complete information regarding titles, dimensions, and dates of execution. Marrozzini's catalog is overly dependent on information provided by the artist's oldest son, which tends to be subjective and incomplete. Orozco's entire output in both drawing and printmaking still awaits a scholarly examination.

Of the nineteen lithographs that Orozco executed in the City of New York, only two depicted exclusively United States subjects—a theater in Harlem and lynched African Americans. The other seventeen prints explore more traditional Mexican subjects. In these, he avoids the folkloric and decorative qualities found in the prints of Rivera, Charlot, Amero, and others. In lithography, as in other mediums, Orozco took popular themes and transformed them into images of pathos and tragedy. The artist's critical and fatalistic view of reality was an antidote to the popular allure of an exotic Mexico.

THE
NEW SCHOOL
FOR SOCIAL
RESEARCH MURAL,
1930-31

Orozco's mural for the New School for Social Research, *A Call for Revolution and Universal Brotherhood*, has generally been considered an aesthetic failure by those who have written about it, from art critic Edward Alden Jewell in 1931 to art historian Laurance Hurlburt in 1989.[1] But is it a failure, or is it an overly ambitious yet unresolved project? In this chapter, I will look at this mural through various contexts: architectural, Orozco's own political aesthetics, the ideas of the Delphic Circle, and his interpretation of Jay Hambidge's Dynamic Symmetry.

Orozco started doing pencil studies (figs. 33–36) on paper for the New School mural during his cross-country railroad journey from California to New York in late September 1930. He had recently completed his first mural in the United States, the *Prometheus* mural at Pomona College, Claremont, California. He began painting at the New School on November 1, 1930, and finished in the early days of January 1931. The murals were dedicated on January 19.[2] The origins of the commission are by now

legendary: Alma Reed arranged an appointment with Dr. Alvin Johnson, the director of the New School, through Lewis Mumford, who was a lecturer at the New School and an admirer of Orozco.[3] Thomas Hart Benton recalled the genesis of the murals at the New School in his 1969 memoirs:

> As Alma was also hunting mural space in order to introduce Orozco to New York, this subject of walls was continually discussed among the three of us. The problem, as I saw it, was not only to find the walls but patrons willing to pay for what we put on them. It was Alma's view that it would be necessary to do the first murals for little or no compensation, in order to win approval of architects. I could not agree with this. . . . However, as it turned out, Alma was right. At this time Alvin Johnson, founder of the New School for Social Research, had raised enough money for the erection of a building for the school on West Twelfth Street near Fifth Avenue. Hearing of this, Alma visited Johnson and offered Orozco's services as a muralist. They were accepted. Orozco would paint a mural for the New School's dining room for the expense of execution. Alma did not inform me of this arrangement.[4]

After the completion of the murals, Reed made it perfectly clear to Johnson that she was in effect the donor:

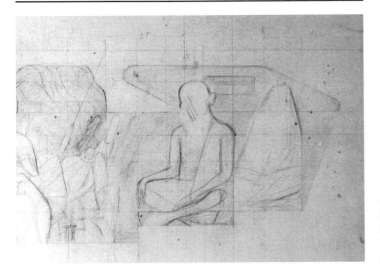

FIGS. 33 (FACING PAGE) AND 34:
Sketches for the New School
for Social Research murals,
1930, pencil on paper.
Instituto Cultural Cabañas.

And it is only right and proper that this cheerfully assumed (though at the time very difficult) responsibility of making it possible for Sr. Orozco to meet his personal and family needs during the progress of the work at the New School remain [*sic*] my own, since the whole idea of frescoes for the New School originated in my own mind; because the work itself represents profoundly my own point of view and idealism, and because, with the Mexican panel my name will be associated with Mexican history.[5]

Again, Benton was overjoyed at the possibility of his first public wall:

So I found my first public wall. Unfortunately, the news of this was received very frigidly by Alma, who felt that I had taken advantage of the opportunity she had found for Orozco to provide one for myself. I must add here that this situation did not affect my relations with Clemente Orozco. We always remained on friendly terms.[6]

Johnson charged both Orozco and Benton to select subjects in contemporary life.[7] Orozco chose anti-imperialist struggles in the Occident and Orient, while Benton settled on the various industries and popular culture of the United States.

The Architectural Context

For Orozco, the particular situation at the New School became a part of his conflict with architecture. In 1929, he had written: "Already the architecture of Manhattan is a new value. . . . The architecture of Manhattan is the first step. Painting and sculpture must certainly follow as inevitable second steps."[8]

The New School building was ideal: it was new and modern. The building had been designed by Joseph Urban, an architect born in Austria who earned his living as a set designer for Florenz Ziegfield. Urban's stylistic allegiance lay with the more expressionistic Wiener Werkstätte, yet the New School building has been described numerous times as a Bauhaus design.[9] The building is more anti-Bauhaus than anything else, however; it may have a Bauhaus surface, but it lacks its substance. A very conservative use of solid brick is balanced in the facade by an aggressive use of horizontals, clearly seen in the wraparound windows, which are Bauhaus-like. The horizontal element was soon to be used as a sign of the International Style in buildings. This horizontality is conveyed in the low ceiling of the dining room, in the dark wainscoting, and in Orozco's own work. In this case, the architectural qualities of the building are reinforced and matched by the architectural dialogue of the frescoes.

Joseph Urban's architecture is, philosophically speaking, Nietzschean in that it is expressionistic, containing a vitalistic quality that was meant to affect those who came in contact with the building in a positive manner. So were some of the philosophical components of the ashram, which may have been derived in part from the architect Henry Van de Velde and his synthesis of Nietzschean philosophy and primitive Hellenism. In view of the whole Nietzschean influence on artists between 1900 and 1925, it is therefore not surprising to see that Nietzsche's theory of abstracted energy appearing in such diverse forms is conveyed through horizontality. Nietzsche's ideas provided justification for a cultural turn from representation to the abstraction of architecture, from the folkloric and ethnocentric to the universal.[10]

FIGS. 35 (FACING PAGE) AND 36: Sketches for the New School for Social Research murals, 1930, pencil on paper. Instituto Cultural Cabañas.

Orozco's Political Aesthetics and the Delphic Circle

From the very start of his career as an artist, Orozco rejected the folkloric *indigenismo* of Rivera and the less talented majority of third-rate members of the Mexican mural movement. For Orozco, Rivera depicted the Mexican Indian in a folkloric manner and in effect exploited the subject:

> What he [Rivera] does by putting a profusion of Indians in his pictures is to make hay while the smallpox rages, a disease that is making our politicians itch. . . . As art for export it is understandable, but there is no excuse for painting it in Mexico.[11]

Unlike Orozco, Siqueiros developed a very specific theoretical response to Rivera's *indigenismo*—a synthesis of the futurist's dynamic sense of form, the plasticity of film (from Sergei Eisenstein), and his own experimental Marxist aesthetics (even though politically he would always be an ally of Stalinism).

Orozco, on the other hand, was by nature antitheoretical and rejected any systematic posing on the part of the artist. Of course, the one exception to this was his involvement with Dynamic Symmetry in the New School panels. Orozco rejected Rivera's folklorism by temporarily embracing the Pythagoreanism of Jay Hambidge's system of Dynamic Symmetry. For Orozco, the choice lay between what Charlot called "plastic values versus descriptive powers."[12] Pythagoreanism already had a place in the cultural context that preceded the mural movement; José Vasconcelos, called by Charlot "the deus ex machina of the Mexican renaissance," as secretary of public education, wrote a philosophical treatise entitled *Pitagoras* while living in exile in 1919.[13] In it he argued that the Greek philosophers, particularly Pythagoras, claimed that art always contains a soothing and therapeutic effect over the passions and daily routines of people, especially when the art bases itself on an ordered system for its expression.[14] This idea, which Orozco must have been aware of before he left for the United States in 1927 (he would always be interested in Vasconcelos as a philosopher), was simply reinforced when he encountered the Delphic Circle ashram of Eva Sikelianos and Alma Reed. I have already mentioned the intellectual presence of Nietzsche in the Delphic program. This program had a lot in common with the political philosophy that the Spanish (and very Nietzschean) writer José Ortega y Gassett had been developing since the 1900s. Simply put, it called for the development of a powerful intellectual elite that would bring both social justice and cultural enlightenment to the masses.[15]

The sociopolitical program of the Delphic Festival—today available only in fragments, with the exception of a French edition—fits in with this Nietzschean/Ortega y Gassett platform. The Delphic Festival was created by the poet Angelos Sikelianos and held in Delphi, Greece. It integrated theater, music, and the visual arts, which were seen as a way of revitalizing a decadent Western civilization. Considering his reaction against Mexican curios, however, Orozco would have rejected the Delphic program's call for a revival and maintenance of local crafts.[16]

Hambidge's Dynamic Symmetry

In his autobiography, Orozco writes regarding the New School panels:

> This painting has the particularity of being con-
> structed according to the geometric-aesthetic prin-
> ciples of the scholar Jay Hambidge. Apart from the
> purely personal realization, I desired to know prac-
> tically up to what point were the principles true
> and useful, and what were their possibilities.[17]

Orozco met Mary Hambidge, widow of Jay Hambidge, at the Sikelianos-Reed apartment. Jay Hambidge had died in 1928, and Mary proposed to Orozco that they continue the development of Dynamic Symmetry together. Orozco explored thoroughly what Hambidge meant in his theory from an understanding of the golden section (see chapter 2). For Hambidge, dynamic structures consist of surfaces organized in geometric proportion, where the relation between the diagonal and the cube are key to the defini-tion of two types of art: the dynamic and the static.[18] The dynamic is best exemplified by the mature periods of both the Egyptians and the Greeks, while the static is the art produced by other cultures, with no exceptions. Works are dynamic because within their forms they have a structure that contains the principle of action, movement, and growth and which develops a structure that multiplies the forms in a way similar to the human body and all living things. These forms, when developed normally, produce a rhythm and a harmony that we define as beautiful.[19] Static art, on the other hand, is composed of passive elements that correspond to the inanimate structures of the world.

Orozco saw Dynamic Symmetry as a strong influence in the United States and Europe beginning in 1920 and ending in 1930: "There wasn't a painter, sculptor, architect or deco-rator, that did not apply in their work the methods of Hambidge; but as it always happens, they were badly inter-preted and became an academic recipe."[20] Perhaps Dynamic Symmetry was for Orozco what classicism was for Picasso, Severini, Derain, and others after World War I. It was a search for a structured way of working and a reaction against the previous aesthetic waves that had been more experimental and less anchored in traditional classical notions of art.[21]

Another possible encounter for Orozco with a direct application of Dynamic Symmetry in a pictorial work may have been through Boardman Robinson's mural sketches for the Kaufmann family's Pittsburgh department store. Robinson (1876–1952) taught at the Art Students League of New York (1924–30) and exhibited sketches for the Pittsburgh murals there in 1929.[22] Orozco, who had exhibited at the league in the spring of the same year, must have seen Robinson's experiment with Dynamic Symmetry. Orozco was not directly influenced by the Pittsburgh murals, yet his encounter with them must have added notions to his thinking concerning the pictorial applications of Dynamic Symmetry.

The New School murals measure eighty square meters of wall space, counting *Science, Labor, Art* (fig. 37), the introductory panel outside the seventh-floor refectory. Inside, the north panel contains the *Table of Universal Brotherhood* (fig. 38); on the east wall is *Struggle in the Orient, Gandhi and Imperialism* (fig. 39); and on the west wall is *Struggle in the Occident, Felipe Carrillo Puerto of Yucatán and Soviet Russia* (fig. 40). The south wall gives us one of Orozco's few tender moments, *Home* (fig. 41). All of the panels stress horizontality and contain a color scheme dominated by browns, reds, oranges, and ochers, as well as a great deal of blue after recent conservation.

Since the murals are located in a small space, the manipulation of scale becomes a dominant issue and a factor in the transmission of meaning. Orozco, in fact, altered Hambidge's Dynamic Symmetry in these frescoes. Orozco's figures fit the human body into an architectural structure. Their meaning is imposed from outside by form rather than from within by the meaning of each figure. The formal result of Orozco's approach is a painting style that charges with tension the architectural space. In contrast to Rivera's scale, which is fixed and in turn fixes the spectator into a single position, Orozco consistently uses a shifting scale, which makes the spectator, not the building, the active participant in the visual dialogue. Orozco

FIG. 37: *Science, Labor, Art*, 1931, fresco. The New School for Social Research. Photograph by KONY.

emphasizes the geometric structure of forms, specifically human forms, instead of the architectural value of the painting as a whole.

Justino Fernández, in his 1942 *Orozco forma e idea*, considers the New School murals "at first glance cubistic" and says the composition "has a sense of geometry, repetition, which makes the paintings tight, stretched, a bit hard." Elsewhere, he finds the drawing more stiff than in Orozco's other work. Although Fernández does bring up Dynamic Symmetry, he simply accepts that Orozco used it whole, not critically. He interprets the New School murals as Orozco's subjection to architecture, where the abstract essence of the composition fits into the proportions of the space. Fernández finds in the panels a few emotional touches, particularly evident in the naturalistic portraits.[23] In the end, the formalist Fernández cannot see into the forms of the New School murals.

Luis Cardoza y Aragón, the Guatemalan poet and art

critic, also misses the essence of the New School murals. In his 1959 *Orozco*, he writes: "When he works basing himself on the theories of Hambidge, as in the murals in the New School for Social Research in New York, he limits instead of expanding himself. Orozco was aware of this. In him it is not the rule but the exception to the rule." Cardoza y Aragón understood Orozco's work as a "baroque expressionism," and any involvement on the artist's part with a method (even if he was subverting it) undermines this notion.[24]

The misunderstanding regarding the New School murals continued into the 1950s with MacKinley Helm's 1953 *Man of Fire: J. C. Orozco*. Helm found the murals loose and bleak, richer in theme than form, and generally disappointing. For Helm, the domestic panel *Home* is gloomy. He concludes: "It was Orozco's nature to be spontaneous, baroque, and ecstatic, and if he continued to admire the classical style as more certainly revealing suggestions of movement to the advanced intellect, it was because Hambidge had unhappily taught him to feel that the ecstatic style is inferior."[25]

Critics misinterpreted and dismissed the New School murals from the start. Yet there were also a handful of champions. Helen Appleton Reade of the *Brooklyn Eagle* wrote: "Strangely enough, . . . [t]he effect of Orozco's portrayal of the revolutionary movement is one of serene peacefulness."[26] Lloyd Goodrich wrote in *The Arts*:

> Orozco's murals furnish a striking contrast to Benton's in almost every respect. They are in a larger room and are in fresco, handled broadly and simply. Their prevailing warm, earthy color, together with the cool gray stone of wainscoting and floor and the plain white of the ceiling, give the whole room a quieter, simpler, more primitive effect.

Even after such positive comments, Goodrich ultimately found the murals lacking emotional intensity, their abstract qualities carrying the least conviction.[27]

Perhaps the most perceptive criticism of the New School murals was written by painter and critic Fairfield Porter. It appeared four years after the murals had been

FIG. 38: *Table of Universal Brotherhood,* 1931, fresco. The New School for Social Research. Photograph by KONY.

unveiled under the title of "Murals for Workers" in the leftist periodical *Arise.* In this article, Porter dismisses Rivera and his influence as mere propaganda. Orozco's New School murals are another matter:

At the head of this class is Orozco. Whether or not he is a painter "for the masses" I do not know. He is quoted as having related how when in Mexico City his frescos were unveiled, two people were killed in the crush. But returning tourists tell you that Mexicans dislike his frescos. Orozco is misunderstood as much by his admirers as by those who dislike his work. You are told that here is a man who paints from a kind of helpless, clumsy passion for art. The truth is that no modern painter is better educated in all things related to his craft. To his original intuition for form relationships, he

FIG. 39: *Struggle in the Orient, Gandhi and Imperialism*, 1931, fresco. The New School for Social Research. Photograph by KONY.

can bring to bear four years of mathematics at Mexico University, two year's [*sic*] experience practicing architecture, two years studying anatomy at medical schools, he has also studied agriculture. . . . Two things determine the quality of the frescos in the dining room for the New School for Social Research: the architecture of the building and the ideas of the mural. This sounds elementary: it is. The austerity of the international style is matched by the angular, bare-bone style of painting. The idea is the revolutionary movement. In the walls about Mexico, India, and Russia, the leaders are realistically painted in contrast to the masses who have group reality rather than individual reality.[28]

For Porter, Orozco "has brought back to painting something that had disappeared: dramatic form."[29]

Forms of Ideology

The narrative of the New School murals is obvious. Orozco made their message clear:

> [I]n the center, the table of universal brotherhood; men of all races presided over by a Negro. On the side walls allegories of world revolution. Gandhi, Carrillo Puerto and Lenin. A group of slaves; another group of workers entering their home after the labor of the day. On a wall outside the dining room an allegory of the sciences and arts.[30]

FIG. 40: *Struggle in the Occident, Felipe Carrillo Puerto of Yucatán and Soviet Russia,* 1931, fresco. The New School for Social Research. Photograph by KONY.

The viewer is very clearly looking at an ideological dialogue (if such a thing is possible) between Nationalism and Communism on the east and west walls, respectively. The resolution of this dialogue is to be found on the north wall in the *Table of Universal Brotherhood*. Outside the room we view intellectual as well as physical labor. According to Reed, Orozco painted general types of what he termed the "despised races" in the *Table of Universal Brotherhood* panel:

> a Mexican peon and a Jew flanking an American negro in the role of presiding officer. On the left are seated five figures—a Chinese Mandarin, a blond Anglo Saxon, a European Nordic, and a fur capped Iranian Kurd, and a turbaned Indian. On the right are seated three solid, block-like forms— a thick-lipped African Negro, a bearded Frenchman with classic features, and another Oriental, with the broad nose and high cheek bones of the Cantonese 'coolie,' to symbolize the Chinese masses, one fourth of the world's population.[31]

There are four recognizable figures seated at the *Table of Universal Brotherhood*; on the right, the bearded French philosopher Paul Richard; on the left, the art critic Lloyd Goodrich with a slight mustache; and next to him, the Dutch poet Leonard Van Noppen. At the head of the table, next to the black man, is another nationalist of sorts, the Jewish painter Reuben Rubin, a Zionist and former Parisian friend of Orozco's nemesis, Diego Rivera.[32] All of these

FIG. 41: *Home*, 1931, fresco.
The New School for Social Research.
Photograph by KONY.

men frequented the ashram.

Obviously, the figures with the true radical overtones at the time the mural was completed were Gandhi and, above all, Lenin. Carrillo Puerto had been martyred a number of years before, and his agrarian socialism had been distorted and absorbed into the then stable Mexican state under the Partido Revolucionario Institucional. Gandhi was in 1930–31 very much the figure that most represented an anti-imperialist posture, a specifically anti-British one in Asia. Yet his radicalism was, it might be said, tempered by his political strategy of passive resistance. Both Carrillo Puerto and Gandhi fit under the umbrella of international liberalism represented by the New School.[33]

Lenin, of course, was another matter. Reed narrates:

> I recall that after submitting to Dr. Johnson the sketch for the Soviet panel, I had several conversations with the educator on its significance, and I carried his questions and Orozco's replies back and forth. Dr. Johnson finally agreed with the painter that the Marxist idea and its leader could hardly be omitted from any realistic appraisal of political trends.[34]

Although Lenin had been dead since 1924, the notion

FIG. 42: *Soviet Russia*, 1931, fresco. The New School for Social Research. Photograph by KONY.

of a violent worldwide revolution was still very much alive in the 1930s, particularly in the United States after the 1929 crash and in the midst of the Depression. At the time Orozco painted the New School murals, the Moscow trials had not started, and Stalin's heavy hand was barely acknowledged beyond the circle of dissidents like Trotsky. Yet Orozco's portrayal of Lenin was not the first in a New York City mural. The first image was created by Hugo Gellert for the Worker's Cooperative in Union Square in 1928. When the Communist Party moved to Thirteenth Street two years later, it was painted out.[35] Although only a photographic record of this image remains, it is possible that Orozco, in New York City since December 1927, might have seen the Gellert mural.

The Lenin that Orozco depicts in *Soviet Russia* (1931; fig. 42) is an image of an image. He is painted in a somber mood, his monumental figure taking up the entire space of a large, rectangular banner. His face, all in ochers and grays, is dark, moody, and intense. Behind him are several red banners and beyond them a kind of rising sun. Below him to his right are the impersonal heads of the Red Army, their eyes barely visible, their bayonets mingled with their red star helmets. Art critic Jewell found this passage a reminder of the Red Star brand of hams featured in Macy's department store.[36] Yet is it not possible that Orozco was being slyly critical by showing us a robotic line of heads that could easily be manipulated by a strong leader? After all, is this not the same Red Army that crushed the left-wing rebellion at the Kronstadt Naval Base in 1921?[37]

To Lenin's left is a line of six Red Guards, with Joseph Stalin in the foreground. The bodies are painted simply and geometrically. All hold hammers in their fists. Orozco has chosen to depict Stalin as one of the Red Guards, not as the leader of the Soviet Union that he was in 1930. Orozco's truer, more personal portrayal of Stalin is visible in his 1936–39 mural *The Carnival of Ideologies* at the Guadalajara governor's palace. Here Stalin is depicted as a sinister, mustachioed buffoon holding a gigantic hammer and sickle while sharing a stage with Hitler and Mussolini.

From Alma Reed to Stanton Catlin and most recently in the work of Laurance Hurlburt, the line of Red Guards in the Lenin panel has been interpreted as the different racial types of the Soviet Union. But how does one explain the black man (next to Stalin) and the Latin American Indian at the end of the line? Neither of these is a racial type found in the Soviet Union. This line of men stands more for an international family of communism than anything else. In this case, Orozco's Lenin with his own Communist brotherhood by his side is a clear antecedent to Rivera's 1932–33 Rockefeller Center mural, the main difference being Orozco's usual misogynistic exclusion of women and Rivera's inclusion of them.

Lenin shares the Occidental panel with Yucatán's Felipe Carrillo Puerto (1874–1924), at the time of his death governor of the Mayan state. Carrillo Puerto had an extramarital affair with Alma Reed and afterward planned to divorce his wife and wed the journalist. Without a doubt, his presence in the New School murals is an homage to Reed, even though there is no denying his importance within the Mexican Revolution.

Felipe Carrillo Puerto was born in Motul, the second of fourteen children of a mestizo merchant family. In his youth he became a modest landowner and learned the Maya vernacular as part of his daily life. Politically, he started out as a liberal Maderista; by the end of his life he was a committed agrarian socialist. By 1914, Carrillo Puerto had become a protégé of the populist governor of Yucatán, General Salvador Alvarado, under whom he started to carry out a statewide campaign of agrarian reform. In 1918, Carrillo Puerto took over the Partido Socialista del Sureste and became the new governor. During his regime, Yucatán distributed more land to the peasants than in any other region in Mexico, with the exception of Morelos under Zapata. This action, among others, made him the enemy of the landowning oligarchy in Yucatán, and eventually they plotted with the de la Huerta rebellion and had him assassinated in 1924. Carrillo Puerto also threatened the central government under Obregón; he was rightly perceived as radically propeasant and agrarian, as well as critical of United States industries.[38]

Carrillo Puerto's violent death made him a natural icon for the Mexican muralists. Rivera painted Carrillo Puerto in 1928 wearing a martyr's gown, bullet holes visible, and eyes open to the viewer at the Secretaría de Educación Pública. At the New School, Orozco painted him from the shoulders up, emerging behind a generalized mass of peasants, all of them women and children with the exception of a soldier holding a rifle and seated to the side. Their faces have been quickly painted with the greatest of economic means; a couple of lines of brown suggest a face. Some of the faces are grotesque, bordering on caricature. Standing between a Maya pyramid and five red banners, Carrillo Puerto looks to the side as if foreseeing the future. He wears a light gray jacket, brown tie, and white shirt. His face, although intense, is not brooding like Lenin's. His light-colored eyes project a look of longing; this is accentuated by the darkness around his eyes. Orozco does not portray him as the peasant leader that he was but rather as a leader of peasants who looks like a middle-class intellectual. Behind the Maya pyramid, the sky ranges from black to a light purple-gray, perhaps a metaphor for an optimistic future.

The panel representing Gandhi and imperialism presents the figures against an orange background. Left to right we see men in chains, painted monochromatically. These are followed by a line of representatives of imperialism: a British soldier, some turbaned native Royal Guards, and a line of six soldiers wearing helmets and gas masks. Then there is Gandhi, sitting on an ocher ground. Slightly behind him sits the poet and National Congress activist Sarojini Naidu. Her entire body is covered by a light-brown, almost orange sari. Together with the Malinche and various peasant women in the murals in the Preparatoria, the depiction of Naidu is one of Orozco's few nonmisogynistic presentations of a woman in a mural. He has not painted her figure at the bottom of the mural nor so much behind Gandhi that she is a figure of total dependency. Her face is quiet and firm; the closed quality of her body evokes strength. Gandhi is depicted cross-legged and dressed in a white loincloth, revealing parts of his torso. As a portrait, Gandhi's face is one of the most realistic portrayals in Orozco's New School mural. His face is pensive, bordering on sadness. From where he is sitting, he confronts the abstracted and mechanical representatives of British imperialism. Reed wrote in 1956 that Orozco seems to have been most "simpatico" to Gandhi and that his feelings inspired the moving portrayal of the Indian Nationalist. In a way, in terms of sensibility Orozco was probably closest to Gandhi among the three revolutionaries portrayed. Like Gandhi, Orozco was an antitechnological man who rejected organized religion while maintaining a very personal spiritual sensibility. In the end, they both favored ethics over ideology.

Formally and conceptually, the weakest part of the New School murals is the allegorical panel in the refectory. The abstract qualities lack Orozco's usual tension. Still, the faces of *Science*, *Labor*, *Art* reveal turbulence and anxiety, as if the order their disciplines are meant to impose on reality is so overwhelming that they become chaotic.

The *Home* panel, which Helm finds "gloomy," is anything but that. In this composition, Orozco reveals a tenderness rarely seen in his art. It is true that the still-life element seems stiff (he lacked Rivera's talent in depicting this subject), yet the overall work is warm without being sentimental. Once again, women are portrayed neither as harlots nor depraved schoolgirls but as strong wives and

FIG. 43: *The Slaves*, 1931, fresco. The New School for Social Research. Photograph by KONY.

mothers. The children are painted simply and directly, though they lack the individual quality found in Rivera's depictions of children.

The most revealing aspect of the New School murals is *The Slaves* (fig. 43) in the Gandhi panel. One of the most disturbing of these figures is the one that has been identified as "the Old Man Throwing Off his Chains."[39] Left unpainted and highly schematized by Orozco, he represents one extreme of the artist's thought on form. Like Hambidge's Dynamic Symmetry, "the Old Man" is not finished; his figure still shows the base construction known as *mise-en-trait*, the French academic practice Orozco had learned at the San Carlos Academy.[40] Orozco explained at one point that his colorless figures in the New School mural were meant to be living in the past.[41] Caught between the enslaved masses and the enslaved native intellectual class, "the Old Man" raises his chains in anger. Against the dark figure of the oppressor, he is a ghostlike white. His rebellion is incomplete. He is a structure without spirit.

In the end, Orozco's interideological dialogue in the New School murals is problematic. As Shifra Goldman has noted, there is little interaction between the people and the great men of history.[42] Carrillo Puerto, Lenin, and Gandhi are interpreted through the Delphic program's notion of leadership. They are the elite that will enlighten those below them.

Yet there is little interaction among all of the figures, the meaningful exception being the family on the north wall.

Still, there is a dialectic in the levels of abstraction with which Orozco has painted each of the figures. The large-scale Carrillo Puerto, Lenin, and Gandhi are realistic, while the other, smaller figures become more abstract. Finally, "the Old Man Throwing Off his Chains" seems to disappear into a few lines. In these frescoes, the idea of abstraction itself carries a meaning. Orozco's painting, instead of "representing" a conflict, embodies it through formal means. This dialectic of realism and abstraction is both real and metaphorical, both a matter of the object represented and the space it occupies. It is very telling that so-called orthodox Marxists simply ignored Orozco's idiosyncratic "forms of ideology."[43]

In the May 22, 1953, issue of the *New York Times*, an article appeared under the heading "New School Keeps Red Mural Hidden." It states:

> The New School for Social Research will keep indefinitely a yellow cotton curtain over the "Revolutionary Violence" section of a mural in the school's cafeteria by the late Mexican artist José Clemente Orozco, because the painting "does not express the philosophy of the faculty," Dr. Hans Simons, president of the school, declared yesterday.[44]

At the height of the McCarthy period, this bastion of liberalism was following the pack with its anti-Communist hysteria. Orozco, the non-Marxist of "Los Tres Grandes," had left behind in the United States a mural with the images of both Lenin and Stalin. The article concluded that the "Soviet panel connects with a Mexican section of the mural depicting the revolutionary leader, Carrillo Puerto, who also became a casualty of the yellow curtain."[45] The newspaper contains a photograph of a staff member of the New School lifting the yellow curtain to reveal the image of Stalin and the men of many races (fig. 44). Both the ideology of form and the forms of ideology had shifted in the post–World War II United States. Abstract expressionism was at its height, and it was being

FIG. 44: *New York Times*, 1953.

depoliticized by its critics. Orozco's radical experiment had fallen victim to the latest political/cultural fashion.

In the end, Goldman's argument regarding the Mexican mural movement fits Orozco's New School mural. Goldman believes that the mural movement matched Frantz Fanon's description of the third stage of postcolonial development. Here, the local population realizes that it must leave behind the past but cannot agree on the path to follow in the fragmented present.[46] This condition is evident in Orozco's murals at the New School, in which the artist turns toward his recent, revolutionary past and finds it closed— thus, the unresolved tensions of this work.

THE MUSEUM OF MODERN ART MURAL, 1940

From May 2, 1932, to February 13, 1934, with the exception of his only trip to Europe in the summer of 1932, Orozco was involved in the execution of murals in the Baker Library at Dartmouth College, Hanover, New Hampshire.[1] In a letter of June 7, 1934, Orozco wrote his wife:

> I am sending by express through Laredo my boxes of books and other things accumulated over the years here. My paints and brushes I will take with me. I cannot wait to see you and the children, also a landscape that is not New York or Hanover. Although these have been positive years for my work, they have not been easy and I want to return home.[2]

Back in Mexico, Orozco would execute the *Catarsis* portable mural in 1934 for the Palacio Nacional de Bellas Artes. Between 1936 and 1939, Orozco would paint what many consider his masterworks in Guadalajara: the auditorium and dome of the University of Guadalajara, *El hombre creador*; the main stairway of the governor's palace, *Hidalgo*; and the murals dealing with the brutal encounter between pre-Columbian Mexico and the Spanish Empire at the Hospicio

Cabañas. These last murals represent Orozco at his most baroque and apocalyptic. In these panels, his vision of both the natives and the Spaniards is brutal and vitriolic; there is no political correctness here. It is also in these murals where Orozco continued to paint a negative view of technology, a view that can be traced to the 1932–34 Dartmouth murals. His one life-affirming moment in the entire cycle is the *Hombre en llamas* (fig. 45), where fire is a metaphor for enlightenment and ascension.

The Artist as Antifascist

Orozco returned to New York City for a week in February 1936. He came to attend, with Siqueiros, the first American Artists' Congress. The congress, a Popular Front antifascist organization, was meeting in part to show solidarity with the legitimate republican government of Spain, which was waging a civil war against the fascists. Both he and Siqueiros were the official representatives of the Liga de Escritores y Artistas Revolucionarios (LEAR) to the congress. Founded in 1934 by Mexican writers and visual artists as part of the Popular Front response to fascism, LEAR had strong ties to the Mexican Communist Party, as well as to smaller and non-Trotskyist socialist organizations. Its founding members were writer Juan de la Cabada, painters Siqueiros and Pablo O'Higgins, printmaker Leopoldo Méndez, and sculptor Luis Arenal.[3]

LEAR functioned from 1934 through 1938, producing the periodical *FRENTE a FRENTE* as its official organ. In its various issues, *FRENTE a FRENTE* contained contributions by its founders, Spanish poet Rafael Alberti, and other European authors such as André Gide, John Strachey, and Heinrich Mann. Siqueiros published in its pages an attack on Rivera entitled "Diego Rivera, pintor de cámara del gobierno de México."[4] The organization, due to its Communist Party connection, had a decidedly anti-Trotsky position; therefore, it was anti-Rivera, who at this time was a strong critic of Stalinism and an ally of Trotsky. Orozco published illustrations of his work in *FRENTE a FRENTE*, as well as his greetings to the American Artists' Congress.[5]

In examining Orozco's work at this time, it is important

FIG. 45 (facing page): *Hombre en llamas*, 1936–39, fresco.

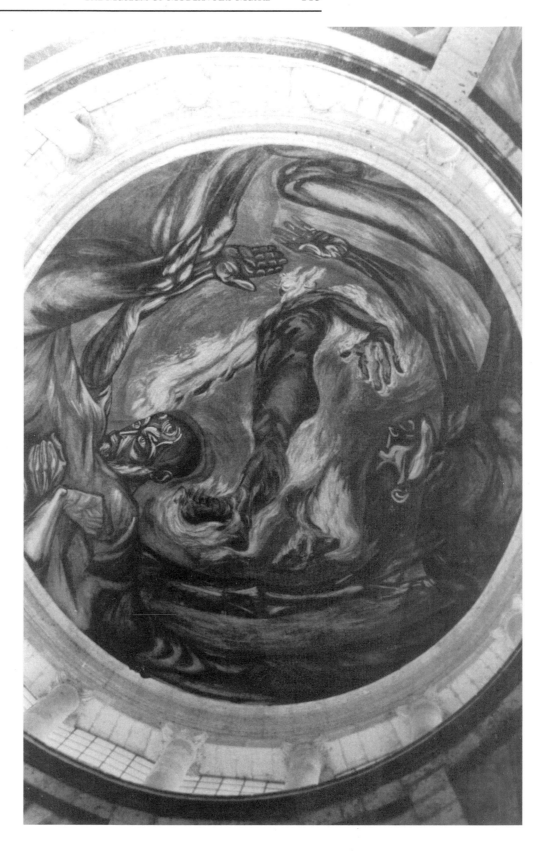

to look briefly at Orozco's politics during this period. Most scholars have either represented him as thoroughly apolitical by the late 1930s or as a misanthropic conservative. Yet here is Orozco active in the Popular Front politics of his time, temporarily forgetting his usual anti-Stalinism and taking on the positions of a typical progressive antifascist. Certainly LEAR's official anti-Rivera stance was also something of an incentive for Orozco's participation.

Orozco once again found himself in New York, this time during the week of February 14, 1936. Although he did not write to his wife, Margarita, as usual, we know he was a Mexican delegate to the congress, read salutations and a general report there, and was "captured" in a caricature by Peppino Mangravite. The American Artists' Congress was among the most important left-wing artistic organizations of the 1930s. This was partly because its policies were actively promoted by Stuart Davis, its national secretary. After the inauguration of the Popular Front in the United States in 1935, the American Communist Party urged the creation of both literary and artistic organizations across the country to aid in the struggle against fascism.[6]

The congress first met February 14–16, 1936, at New York City's Town Hall. It endorsed government art programs and government support for art unions. Its executive committee supported the Stalinist positions on the Spanish civil war and the Finnish-Russian War. By the summer of 1939, the congress came out in support of the Hitler-Stalin pact and the resulting dismemberment of Poland. That year art historian Meyer Schapiro and other anti-Stalinist members abandoned the congress in protest. By 1943, the congress was defunct.[7]

During the final and fourth closed session of the congress, which took place at the New School for Social Research, where his murals were still on view, Orozco read his three-page report to the congress, starting with the salutation "Comrades." He then stated the four points taken up and agreed upon by the LEAR assembly:

> 1. The artist's position as far as the problems of imperialism, Fascism and war are concerned.

2. The economic security for artists, including artists and craftsmen in popular arts as well as artists engaged in teaching.

3. The artists' and workers' organizations.

4. And finally, form and content in art.[8]

As the representative of LEAR, Orozco confined himself to issues of international scope, such as ways of building coalitions of antifascist artists' organizations beyond national borders. Above all, he stressed the "party line" of LEAR, which was similar to that of the Congress: "The artist's means of struggle also include the open revealing of all crimes and criminal attempts practiced against intellectuals and artists in fascist countries, and the waging of an intense campaign against the forces which are leading humanity toward a new massacre." Orozco concluded his report with details regarding the payment of dues to the Mexican artists' union, fund-raising activities, and other matters.[9]

Orozco did not write the document he read. The Popular Front language used throughout it betrays the presence of Siqueiros and possibly Arenal as coauthors of the report, not simply because they were among the founders of the organization but also because both could speak and write the English language. Yet knowing Orozco's highly idiosyncratic personality, he must have had a hand in the writing, otherwise it is doubtful that he would have read it merely as a representative of LEAR.

Following Orozco, Siqueiros read "The Mexican Experience in Art," which was a reflection on the position regarding fascism of the National Assembly of Artists of Mexico, another antifascist organization. In this document, Siqueiros called for a depiction of "daily, popular life," for a formal language that could reach the largest number of people, for teamwork as opposed to isolated and individual work, and, of course, on the economic front, for an accessible art. Siqueiros also called for a solid unity on the questions of defense against the menace of fascism and war, even if the artists held different aesthetic positions.[10]

When Orozco returned to Guadalajara, he started to publish a polemic rag sheet which he entitled *ROJO*. In it, he spoke his mind concerning the arguments between Siqueiros and Rivera—usually agreeing with Siqueiros against Rivera but finally being critical of both for their lack of political independence. He also commented on his most recent mural work in Guadalajara. The tone of the rag sheet was generally antifascist in politics and iconoclastic in art.[11] The periodical lasted for a total of four issues. Still, it is significant that at this time Orozco saw the usefulness of the propaganda pamphlet, not only in the fight against fascism but also as a forum in which to make clear his positions on art vis-à-vis Siqueiros and Rivera.

LEAR, like the American Artists' Congress, dissolved over the clashes between the Stalinist and anti-Stalinist Left. The Mexican organization ceased to exist in 1938, at the height of the conflict between communists and anarchists in the Spanish civil war, a cause very dear to the Mexican intelligentsia.[12] It is not known where Orozco stood in this controversy, yet a Guadalajara mural, *The Carnival of Ideologies* (1936–39), depicts simultaneously an antifascist and anti-Stalinist position.

Orozco "Explains"

As mentioned, Orozco had painted his first portable mural, *Catarsis*, in 1934 at the Palacio Nacional de Bellas Artes (where it faces Rivera's *Man at the Crossroads* re-creation of 1934). His last portable mural, *Juarez y la revolución*, would be executed in 1948 at the Palacio de Chapultepec. In between these two falls *Dive Bomber and Tank*, the portable mural he executed for The Museum of Modern Art in New York during the summer of 1940. *Catarsis* presents an apocalyptic massacre where weapons, prostitutes, and a mob of men all attack each other. Thematically this work relates to *Dive Bomber* with its tensions and exaggerations.

MacKinley Helm describes the origin and execution of *Dive Bomber and Tank* in the following manner:

Orozco was still in the middle of painting the Jiquilpan murals [Gabino Ortíz Library, Michoacán] when he was called to The Museum of Modern Art in New York to paint some portable panels in

connection with an exhibition of three freight car-
loads of ancient and modern Mexican art.[13]

At this point, one might ask: how did Orozco view this
patron, The Museum of Modern Art? In his autobiography,
he writes of discovering in Coney Island a business that
rented fat ladies, bearded women, and dwarfs and that
provided an illustrated catalog for potential customers.[14]
Of course, he is exaggerating to make a point about the
excessive commercialism in the United States; still, it is a
valid one. He then continues in the same breath regarding
The Museum of Modern Art:

> This is nothing in particular, since The Museum of
> Modern Art in New York also rents, for exhibitions,
> lots of paintings that are cubist, surrealist, dadaist,
> Mexican or special combinations of Picasso-
> Braque, Picasso-Rouault, Picasso-Matisse, Picasso-
> Chirico, to choose from for a certain amount a
> week for an exhibition at any club, university, or
> cocktail-party where people want to show off with
> modern art.[15]

In this passage, Picasso is mentioned repeatedly;
Orozco was very conscious of Alfred H. Barr Jr.'s (the founding director of the museum) belief in the supreme importance
of the Spaniard in twentieth-century painting. Here Orozco is
poking fun at the museum as a kind of department store of
modernism, making available all sorts of "special combinations"
to its customers.

The Museum of Modern Art had been interested in
Latin America, Mexico in particular, since its foundation
in 1929. After dedicating its first one-person exhibition to
Matisse in 1930, it made Rivera the subject of its second
one in 1931.[16] When he visited the Soviet Union in the
company of Jere Abbott (his Harvard roommate) from
December 1927 through March 1928, Barr had met
Rivera.[17] For Barr, Rivera had the right modernist pedigree:
he had lived in Paris from 1909 to 1921 and was a practicing
cubist painter from 1913 through 1917.[18] During Barr's
visit to the Soviet Union, he acquired, directly from Rivera,

the drawing *Sawing Rails, Moscow* (1927):

> Suddenly decide I want one of Diego Rivera's draw-
> ings. Find him dressing—but all drawings over at
> Sterenberg's, Whither we go, he having an engage-
> ment there. I take back roll of drawings and choose
> a fine charcoal of men working on railroad tracks
> (30 rubles).[19]

Rivera was for Barr the representative of the Latin
American avant-garde, particularly since at the time of his
retrospective at The Museum of Modern Art in 1931, the
artist was on the "outs" with the Mexican Communist Party.
Barr recommended Rivera to the Rockefellers for the Ra-
dio Corporation of America Building mural after Matisse
had turned down the commission.[20] Barr's favorable view
of Rivera ended on May 9, 1933, when the artist and his
assistants were removed by guards and not permitted to
complete the mural *Man at the Crossroads* because of the
image of Lenin.[21]

By 1940, when *20 Centuries of Mexican Art* was to open
at The Museum of Modern Art, Rivera was no longer the
institution's Latin American artist of choice. The exhibition was one of the many efforts of the Inter-American
Good Neighbor policy spearheaded by Nelson Rockefeller
in preparation for the coming war in Europe. This policy,
which originated in 1938, was meant to counteract the
wooing of Latin American countries by the Axis nations.
Germany and Italy had been successful in gaining the support of Argentina, not to mention the friendly neutrality
of Brazil and Paraguay. Also, according to art critic and
Barr confidante José Gómez Sicre (1916–1991), the political turmoil in Europe made it impossible to organize
exhibitions with European partners or acquire works for
the collection; Rockefeller instead advised Barr to look
south to the Rio Grande and beyond. Orozco was probably chosen as the alternative muralist for this occasion in
hopes that he would not create "a situation" like Rivera's
in 1933. After all, Orozco was the oldest of "Los Tres
Grandes." He was neither a Trotskyist like Rivera nor an
orthodox member of the Communist Party like Siqueiros.

Tamayo was out of the question; the museum needed a muralist. Therefore, Barr and his committee (art dealers Inés Amor and Alberto Misrachi, art historian Stanton Catlin, and others) settled on Orozco. Rivera was represented in the exhibition with a singularly nonpolitical work: a sensuous nude of a black woman entitled *Bailarina arrodillada* from 1939.

In letters to his wife, Orozco presents us with the genesis and execution of *Dive Bomber and Tank*:

> You can imagine how tired I am from the trip and with this New York that is unbearable. But I am fine and happy. I am provisionally in the same hotel where the [Lou and Peggy] Riley's also are. Abbott and they went to receive me at the station, but they went to Pennsylvania while I arrived at The Grand Central. Tuesday the meetings regarding the Mexican exhibition start. Castillo Nájera [Mexico's ambassador to the United States] is coming with other self-important people. The painting in fresco will have to wait since they don't even have a wall yet.[22]

In his next letter to his wife, written eleven days later, he mentions his meeting with Nelson Rockefeller (the Abby Aldrich Rockefeller Fund would pay for the mural) and the promise that the portable plaster panels would be ready for him to start painting the next week.[23] In time, Orozco would work on the preparatory sketches for *Dive Bomber and Tank* for roughly a month in his Manhattan hotel, the St. Moritz. There would be meetings with Barr and "two secretaries" so that notes could be taken for the proper construction of the panels.[24] Orozco never really connected with Barr; he found him "severe and ceremonious, almost as if he is about to say mass, but of course he can't since he really comes across as a Calvinist minister. It is obvious that he believes he possesses the gospel of modernity, with Picasso at the head and followed by the mastodon Rivera."[25]

As Orozco was about to despair due to lack of progress in the preparation of the portable panels, John E. Abbott, executive vice-president of The Museum of Modern Art, took over the arrangements. The artist started to paint *Dive Bomber and Tank* before June 10, 1940.[26]

The structure—with six panels, each measuring nine by three feet—is set up in the lobby of the museum (fig. 46). The public relations department, as well as Barr, encouraged a constant group of onlookers to view the artist at work. Rivera had done this successfully during his 1931 retrospective. This activity was also popular at the New York World's Fair in 1939 and 1940. Orozco cooperated occasionally with this situation but bought screen panels, which he placed around himself and the work when he was tired of being "a monkey eating his peanuts for the entertainment of children."[27] Orozco was assisted by Lewis Rubinstein, a professor of art at Vassar College, who had studied fresco painting in Rome together with Rico Lebrun.[28]

The artists Jacob Lawrence and Bernarda Bryson both visited the museum to watch Orozco paint *Dive Bomber and Tank*. For Lawrence, Orozco "worked carefully and precisely, rarely spoke and had a mischievous smile. I asked if I could do anything for him, and he asked me for a bag of cherries. I came back with it and we shared it, when he stopped painting and took a brief rest. I was mesmerized by his painting, it had plastic values. . . . Form, color, and still it had a narrative."[29] Bryson remembered the process as one of "incredible speed; he used a large sponge to paint the backgrounds, his colors would be mixed in cocktail or tumbler glasses, and I believe he used

FIG. 46: Movable panels for *Dive Bomber and Tank*, 1940.

FIG. 47: Sketch on panels of *Dive Bomber and Tank*, 1940.

hard bristle brushes to paint the details, as opposed to Rivera who preferred sable.... I was amazed at the speed with which Orozco worked, and this with only one hand." In addition, she recalled, "Later on, I went with Ben [Shahn, her husband] to see the completed mural and we were both mesmerized. It was at first sight so ab-

stract, but not really. Ben thought Orozco's painting was moving and genuinely anarchic. Over time he [Shahn] saw Rivera as utopic and simplistic. Siqueiros to him was a loud-mouth Stalinist. The great one was Orozco."[30]

Orozco made no full-size cartoon for *Dive Bomber and Tank*; instead, he drew in pencil to the scale of one inch to one foot.[31] The salient lines were enlarged on the equalizing coat and gone over in red pigment (fig. 47).[32] As usual, Orozco wore a mechanic's jumpsuit when painting (fig. 48), as opposed to Rivera's more "folkloric" overalls. Orozco painted *Dive Bomber and Tank* with minimal assistance from Rubinstein. As Rubinstein stated, "I would assist him with things and mixing paints and colors . . . but essentially the designing of the painting was all his. He would paint very spontaneously. Yes. Often just kind of improvising things as he went along. He spoke fairly good English. He spoke English to get along. And I spoke a little Spanish."[33] Orozco used only lime-proof colors: "earthen colors, Mars colors, cobalt, chromium oxide, non-animal blacks and lime white. Good cadmiums may be used also very thinly. The binding medium is carbonate of lime produced during the drying of the plaster."[34]

Throughout the progress of the mural, artists kept visiting to watch Orozco at work. According to Rubinstein, both Anton Refregier and Philip Guston came by, and he

FIG. 48: Orozco painting *Dive Bomber and Tank*, 1940.

introduced them to Orozco. These two artists invited Orozco to come to a hall downtown and speak to a group of American muralists. Orozco agreed but eventually stood them up.[35]

On July 5, 1940, Orozco wrote to his wife announcing the conclusion of the mural (fig. 49). He was still awaiting final payment—a total of $7,500 for the project—as well as his imminent return to Mexico via Havana.[36] Yet before he could return to his family, the painter had to write a didactic brochure in which he would explain the technical process of fresco painting and the concept behind *Dive Bomber and Tank*. Barr had requested this brochure.[37]

In a matter of days, Orozco wrote the text that would be reproduced in the twelve-page pamphlet *Orozco "Explains."* The pamphlet includes nine photographs of the artist at work and eleven of the mural in progress, from genesis to conclusion. The text contains technical passages by Orozco and the main body of the text, where he "explains." He starts in a sarcastic tone:

> The public wants explanations about a painting. What the artist had in mind when he did it. What was he thinking of. What is the exact name of the picture, and what the artist means by that. If he is glorifying or cursing. If he believes in Democracy.[38]

He continues:

> And now the public insists on knowing the plot of modern painted opera, though not Italian, of course. They take for granted that every picture must be an illustration of a short story or of a thesis and want to be told the entertaining biography and bright sayings of the leaders in the stage-picture, the ups and downs of hero, villain, and chorus. . . . Suddenly, Madame Butterfly and her friend Rigoletto disappear from the stage-picture. Gone, too, are gloomy social conditions. To the amazement of the public the curtain goes up and nothing is on. The Abstract. The public protests and demands explanations, and explanations are given freely and generously. Rigoletto and social conditions are still

FIG. 49: Orozco completing *Dive Bomber and Tank*, 1940.

there but have become abstract, all dolled up in cubes and cones in a wild surrealist party. . . . The public refuses to SEE painting. They want to HEAR painting. They don't care for the show itself, they prefer TO LISTEN to me barker [*sic*] outside. Free lectures every hour for the blind, around the Museum. This way please.[39]

Orozco has essentially written a farce where he ridicules The Museum of Modern Art's definitions and explanations of modern painting. He is skeptical of the museum's trying to present the artist "at work," involved in the act of creation with great "sincerity," all for the enlightenment of the "public":

The Artist must be sincere. It is true. He must be sincere. The actor on stage commits suicide to thrill or frighten the public to death. The actor feels exactly what a suicide feels, and acts the same way except that his gun is not loaded. He is sincere as an artist only. Next week, he has to impersonate

St. Francis, Lenin or an average business man, very sincerely.[40]

At the close of the pamphlet, Orozco co-opts the language of formalist modernism:

> A painting is a Poem and nothing else. A poem made of relationships between forms as other kinds of poems are made of relationships between words, sounds or ideas.
>
> Sculpture and architecture are also relationships between forms. This word forms includes color, tone, proportion, line, etcetera.[41]

In the end, he disturbs ahistorical formalism by bringing up history and human beings:

> A linotype is a work of art, but a linotype in motion is an extraordinary adventure affecting the lives of many human beings or the course of history. A few lines from a linotype in action may start a World War or may mean the birth of a new era.[42]

Orozco subverts formalist notions of art by using a formal language but not meaning any of it. He knew that art could only affect society in an indirect and complicated manner. Yet he used the positive language of a "linotype in action," and we know full well that long ago he gave up any simplistic belief in the salvific qualities of art. Still, Orozco knew what was expected of him. Unlike Rivera, who was optimistic in his California and Detroit murals and had high expectations of "liberal" United States institutions, Orozco "performed" in the language of formalism, consciously, sarcastically. To him, formalism was as corrupt and defunct as the technology (which had given patrons wealth) that had supported it—the technology we see in the paintings of the precisionists and Rivera's Detroit murals.

Near the last pages of the pamphlet, six photographs present the original arrangement of *Dive Bomber and Tank* (the way the artist painted it), plus five variations in which the panels can be rearranged. The rearrangements do not work (fig. 50). They are also part of Orozco's verbal farce. He knew that the museum's administration believed in

FIG. 50: Several arrangements of *Dive Bomber and Tank*, 1940.

FIG. 51: *Dive Bomber and Tank*, 1940, fresco, 9 x 18 ft. on six panels 9 x 3 ft. each.
The Museum of Modern Art, New York. Commissioned through the Abby Aldrich Rockefeller Fund.
Photograph © 1997 The Museum of Modern Art, New York.

the innate abstract qualities of a work and the ability of these qualities to make the work function from any angle. Orozco demonstrates to us that the mural works only one way, the way he painted it, thereby undermining formalism with its own technique.

The Machine as Apocalyptic Hell

With a palette of grays, blues, purples, black, and touches of red-orange, *Dive Bomber and Tank* measures nine by eighteen feet, with each of the panels individually measuring nine by three feet. The subject of this mural can be read as a dive bomber crashed into a tank, surrounded by chained heads, while on the sides are human and mechanical refuse (fig. 51). The background is silvery, infinite gray with washes of pale blue, evoking an endless space. Orozco was painting this mural roughly at the time that the German forces were entering Paris. He was probably aware of the Stuka bombers, as the Nazis called them. No doubt this informs the background of the mural. The work is an allegory against war, informed by the artist's "invisible" and iconoclastic anarchism. Yet it is more than a critique of the situation of the summer of 1940. *Dive Bomber and Tank* is a critique of progress in its most mechanical, industrial sense. It is an antitechnological mural. It is an antiwar mural also, not against a specific war but war in general. Formally, it is the earliest example of the artist's exploration of abstraction; this work makes possible later works such as the *Alegoría nacional* mural in 1947–48 and easel works such as *Esclavo* and *Paisaje metafísico*, both in 1948.

How should we interpret *Dive Bomber and Tank*? Despite Orozco's denial about artists having any political convictions, we must go to his politics, even though they are distant and invisible, to read this portable mural. Remember that only four years earlier, in the very city where he would paint *Dive Bomber and Tank*, Orozco had represented LEAR at the American Artists' Congress. On this occasion, we have the artist as antifascist, not as an apolitical cynic.

By 1940, however, the cultural/political landscape had already started to shift, and Orozco, in weaving his own myth, went in the opposite direction of Rivera and

Siqueiros. They emphasized their politics, while he wanted to make his politics invisible. Again, Orozco knew the rules of the game and would play them to get the work done. He had no interest in scandals and canceled commissions like Rivera or periods of incarceration like Siqueiros. He wanted to subvert through the work.

As previously stated, Orozco's only known political affiliation was with the anarcho-syndicalism of the Casa del Obrero Mundial. His widow recalled seeing a copy of Ricardo Flores Magón's writings and an anthology of anarchist texts among his books.[43] Anarchists reject the idea of any state (whether of the Left or Right), believe in a grassroots workers' democracy, and reject all war as a creation of the powerful elites for the maintenance of their power.[44] Both Cardoza y Aragón and Gómez Sicre maintained that Orozco was basically an anarchist. Throughout the years that both critics knew Orozco, the artist made derogatory remarks not just about the opportunism of Rivera and the dogmatic communism of Siqueiros, but also about the heartless capitalism of the United States and the brutality of fascism.[45]

Justino Fernández interprets *Dive Bomber and Tank* as "the very being of the life of today, charged with fear, oppression, danger, of materialism and mechanization, a life of refuse and constant flow." He adds that, stylistically, the artist was absorbing both Byzantine and cubist influences and points to the angular aspects of the composition and fragmentation of forms as proof.[46] Cardoza y Aragón cannot see *Dive Bomber and Tank* as anything but an unsuccessful incursion into abstraction.[47] MacKinley Helm, like Cardoza y Aragón, misses Orozco's point regarding this work:

> I was in Mexico City myself, at the time, and I wrote up to New York to ask him to tell me what he meant to do there so that, though I perhaps would not see it, I could speak of the painting in my forthcoming book. He replied on June 21, 1940, that the subject matter of the work would be "something like an airplane for war or a tank, with some figures. It would have no meaning except the one that the spectator

may think it has."[48]

Later on, Helm criticizes the mural as having weak forms, an uneven concept, and a cold palette. He dismisses the work as Orozco's forced attempt at pleasing the formalist aesthetic of The Museum of Modern Art.[49] Helm is wrong; Orozco, very conscious of the institution's aesthetic, uses and subverts it.

In 1991, The Museum of Modern Art exhibited *Dive Bomber and Tank*, which had been in storage since 1946. On this occasion, the mural was reproduced in full color in the accompanying publication.[50] The following text appeared in the publication's checklist:

> Orozco's mural Dive Bomber and Tank was painted two months after Dunkirk. His mind, like ours, was full of the shock of the mechanical warfare which had just crushed western Europe. But instead of picturing an actual incident with technically accurate details, he makes us feel the essential horror of modern war—the human being mangled in the crunch and grind of grappling monsters "that tear each other in their slime." We can see suggestions of the bomber's tail and wings, of tank treads and armor plate and human legs dangling from the jaws of shattered wreckage.
>
> Beneath emerge three great sightless masks weighed with chains which hang from pierced lips or eyes. These ancient symbols of dramatic agony and doom are fused with the shapes of modern destruction to give the scene a sense of timeless human tragedy.[51]

This highly literary and World War II-specific interpretation comes out of Barr's *What Is Modern Painting?* (1946).[52] Barr divested the painting of any profound political connection and interprets it only in the light of a recent event (Dunkirk). He edits out Orozco's genuinely apocalyptic view of technology, a technology that is the product of capitalism.

Orozco himself was both clear and evasive in his explanations of the *Dive Bomber and Tank* mural. The *New*

York Herald Tribune reported that the artist explained the general theme of the work as "the subjugation of man by the machines of modern warfare, but he is less definite about the various objects in the design, which he said represented whatever the observer chooses to see in them."[53] To the *New York Times*, Orozco sounded blatantly apolitical:

> According to the artist, his selection of the subject has no political significance. He wished to paint an aspect of modern life. "That is what modern art is," Mr. Orozco explained when the commission was announced, "the actual feeling of life around us or the mood of whatever is just happening."[54]

Here once again we encounter the sly, farcical language of the *Orozco "Explains"* pamphlet.

Dive Bomber and Tank is a more abstract continuation of the antimachinery sensibility that we can see in the Dartmouth and *Catarsis* murals, as well as the Hospicio murals of 1936–39 in Guadalajara. Behind its content is the artist's anarchist past, activism in LEAR, and even his future signing of international peace petitions.[55]

In *Dive Bomber and Tank*, Orozco's aesthetic program stands in complete opposition to Rivera's, as evident in the *Detroit Industry* and *Man at the Crossroads* murals. Rivera is clear in his formal language, didactic in narrative, and optimistic when it comes to the possibilities of machinery in the revolution of the future. Orozco, in this work, is a true allegorist—tragedy is evoked through the symbolic use of both masks and machines, as well as through his use of dramatic angles and extreme light in the mural, which transform the composition into a baroque pictorial statement. The machine and the system that produced it are essentially misanthropic.

José Clemente Orozco left from Mexico City for what would be his last visit to New York on September 15, 1945. Partly vacation but mostly business trip, the artist was once again looking for a gallery in New York City, as well as further exposure in the post-World War II art market.[1] After being in the city a few days, he wrote to his wife, Margarita, letting her know he was staying at the Yacht Club on West Forty-fourth Street, that he had been attending openings and the theater, and that he was healthy, even after the long train ride. He added that everywhere he went, people asked him about Alma Reed, who seemed to have disappeared.[2] By his second letter to her, he was settled in a one-bedroom apartment on 6 East Seventy-ninth Street, had purchased canvas for painting, was sticking to a vegetarian diet, and found New York too fast, filled with people everywhere and very expensive.[3]

On October 17, he wrote again to Margarita, laying out his plan of work and making some acute observations:

> I am going to use the small living room as a temporary studio, and I will concentrate on producing a few easel works. Possibly some landscapes of the city, a self-portrait, etc., we'll see.
>
> Recently I encountered Tamayo at the house of a collector, he barely spoke to me; his wife is quite vulgar. It seems that his work has quite a

market in New York now. He is not a bad painter, although too decorative for my taste. I am going to talk to the people at Knoedler. As I wrote to you before, the Knopf publishing house asked Paul Westheim to write my biography, yet he has not done anything. I want to interest them in publishing the autobiography. Mural painting seems to be completely dead here, the fashion has changed and now easel painting and abstraction seems to be the thing. It is already cold. I am fine and eating well. I can make breakfast here.[4]

Once again, Orozco made contact with John Abbott of The Museum of Modern Art, who introduced him to Julien Levy. Orozco liked Levy, yet knowing that Jean Charlot exhibited with him, he asked his wife to inquire with Charlot regarding Levy's ethics as a dealer. He continued to talk to Levy, but nothing concrete came out of the conversations. He was aware that in November there would be exhibitions of Tamayo, Mérida, and Siqueiros and that the public still loved decorative pictures filled with Indians.[5] He had a pleasant surprise when he finally visited The Museum of Modern Art:

> In the Museum of M. A. The zapatistas are hanging, and in their shop they have a wonderful color reproduction. It costs 3 doll. I am going to buy it. They also have Alma's monograph of me. I don't know if I should buy it.[6]

By the end of October, Orozco started to express concerns regarding his expenses in New York City. He did not think that he would be able to stay too long and asked his wife to request payment for the portrait that he had finished of the archbishop of Mexico City, Mons. Luis María Martínez.[7] In November, he received a letter from Knoedler:

> Yesterday I received a letter from Knoedler, a copy of which I enclose. I will respond accepting and this is the equivalent of a formal contract. . . . Now I only have to do my best and for this I have to work hard, since from this depends my getting at-

tention as an easel painter. The public still believes that I am only a mural painter and to this belief have contributed Inés [Amor, owner of the Galeria de Arte Méxicano] and her minor painters, in bad faith and to their benefit.[8]

From 1946 until his death, Knoedler would handle Orozco's easel paintings, yet the gallery never did give him a one-person exhibition.[9] The one Mexican artist the gallery promoted constantly at this time and into the 1950s was Rufino Tamayo.[10]

Orozco visited exhibitions, just as he did when he was in the city in the late 1920s and 1930s. He was disappointed with the recent drawings of Matisse and found them boring and too simplistic, yet he could still sense a major painter at work.[11] He went to a Siqueiros exhibition at Pierre Matisse:

Siqueiros at Pierre Matisse: lithographs from last year, easel paintings. A good self-portrait. He is a good painter, very dynamic. Powerful forms. It is a shame he wastes so much time talking and with communism.[12]

At the end of November 1945, in the "Talk of the Town" section of *The New Yorker*, Orozco was highlighted:

José Clemente Orozco, the Mexican painter is living and working in two rooms on the fifth floor rear of the old William Carter Dickerman house at 6 East Seventy-ninth Street. He came here three months ago and got his present lodgings by answering an ad. "I arrived early in the morning ahead of everyone else," he told us when we called on him last week. "First I stayed at the New York Yacht Club, where a friend of mine got a friend of his, who was a member, to get a room for me. My friend could not get me a hotel room." . . . We asked Orozco whether he had run into many of the members. "Most of the members are admirals," he said, "and they are all away in the service."[13]

In this passage, we can read Orozco's dry sense of humor still very much at work. The article continued:

Orozco hasn't seen any snow for ten years and hopes to paint some this winter. He works whenever he feels rested, sometimes in the morning, sometimes in the middle of the night, and averages eight hours a day. He has a cot in his studio, a cot and a bed in his bedroom, and a small table and four straight armless chairs. He likes to visit the Metropolitan and Frick museums and to eat at the Brussels. "Facts are always distorted," he said, showing us some distorted sketches of the devil. "I'd like to show life as it is, but art is not a document, not a record, not scientific research; it is a philosophy."[14]

By early December, Orozco was complaining to Margarita about the lack of money, the cold weather, and the daily anxieties of living in a city that he barely recognized. He found it difficult to work at painting; he lacked the necessary peace of mind.[15] According to the correspondence with his wife, Orozco painted several allegorical-symbolic oils of "the destruction of civilization," some small landscapes of New York City under the snow, and a self-portrait during his 1945–46 stay in the city.[16] The location of the landscapes and symbolic works are unknown, while the self-portrait has been for many years in the collection of the Carrillo Gil Museum in Mexico City.

Autorretrato (fig. 52), started at the end of 1945 and finished in early 1946, would be the artist's last finished self-portrait. Measuring thirty-five by thirty inches, it is signed on the center right of the canvas: J. C. Orozco/N.Y. 1946. Orozco depicts himself right in the foreground of the picture plane, giving his body the massive shoulders it did not have in life. He wears a dark gray suit with touches of green and blue. The background has been broken into a dark pyramid shape, painted thinly in a dark Prussian blue that is almost black. Juxtaposed next to it is another pyramid shape, this one painted thickly in a tan-yellow. Next to it is a vertical rectangle, loosely painted in a bluish-gray. Orozco has drawn his head vigorously, emphasizing his forehead, cheekbones, and chin. His thick glasses are painted in purple, black, and brown; behind the lenses we see his

FIG. 52: *Autorretrato*, 1946, oil on canvas. Museo de Arte Alvar y Carmen T. de Carrillo Gil.

small, intense greenish eyes. The entire face is comprised of colorful pink, green, crimson, and yellows, juxtaposed against the brownish flesh. The mustache is gray with touches of purple. Throughout the entire painting, he juxtaposes thick and thinly painted areas, creating a balance between the two on the surface. The expression is intense and serious. The head and shoulders become a compact form pressing against the viewer. He depicts himself as a formal person wearing a suit and tie. Yet the face goes beyond this representation. Here is Orozco as an older man, filled with a critical vision of reality, a man still in the plenitude of his powers.

Margarita joined Orozco in New York City in early February 1946. She brought more than twenty recent drawings, as well as a few large paintings on masonite. They were consigned to Knoedler, where Orozco was supposed to have an exhibition in October 1946.[17]

On February 13, Orozco was interviewed by art critic and curator José Gómez Sicre for the magazine *Norte*, a Spanish-language cultural monthly published under the auspices of the United States Information Agency. Gómez Sicre never published the interview; his editor, Jorge Losada, found it anti-American, or rather anti-United States.

Gómez Sicre asked Orozco a number of key questions, and Orozco responded honestly:

You came here in 1927 looking for artistic opportunities?

Yes, the mural commissions had dried up, so I came to the United States. I spent seven years here, they were difficult, I didn't make much money, yet they were important for my work as a painter. When I came here Mexico was the fashion. Everyone wanted pretty pictures of Indians. Now they like Tamayo.

What about your paintings of New York scenes?

I never liked the industrial forms of the city, be it underground trains, skyscrapers or anything else. I did use them as themes for paintings, not just because of the powerful forms but because it was the reality around me, what I knew. You know my paintings of New York were not well received, they wanted me to paint Indians with flowers, like Rivera. I think I captured something of the brutality of the city in those New York paintings, they are not pretty pictures.

Maestro, the last time you were in the city, almost six years ago, you painted the mural *Dive Bomber and Tank* at The Museum of Modern Art. What is this work about?

I wrote a small pamphlet for the museum where I explained what the work is about . . . [he laughs]. . . . It is about war, the terror of the world then, today and tomorrow.

How do you see the world situation?

It is important that fascism was defeated. But now we have other tensions. I am a little afraid of a pax americana, at least as it refers to Latin

America. Let me emphasize that I am not political like Rivera and Siqueiros.

How different do you find the New York of today from the one you knew before?

Very different, in the thirties even with the economic crisis there was a different atmosphere. There was an interest in mural painting that is no longer. Today the interest is in easel painting and abstraction.

Do you think you will return to New York?

I don't believe so.[18]

This unpublished interview gives us an idea of the artist's frame of mind and way of speaking during his last visit to New York City. Although he was clear in his statements, he was at the same time concealing, criticizing the United States while stressing that he was not political like Rivera and Siqueiros. As in one of the letters to his wife, here he mentions touristic Indian pictures in the same breath as Tamayo. For Orozco, Tamayo's pseudoabstractions were essentially folkloric commodities that Anglo collectors liked to hang in their living rooms. Yet when Gómez Sicre asked him about his time in New York, in spite of his criticisms he considered the time vital to his work as a painter.

On March 14, 1946, Orozco was back in Mexico City with Margarita.[19] He would never again set foot in Gringoland, although his name continued to be a part of the cultural discourse in the United States. In the summer of 1947, *Time* printed a short article where Orozco was quoted. Italian author Giovanni Papini had made statements to the press that Latin America had not produced anything of importance and influence in the realm of culture. *Time* reported:

Boomed painter José Clemente Orozco, an old hand at cultural warfare: "Papini is the type that believes that Paris is the unique city where all culture has been centralized. His attitude is that of commercialized Europe, of the French dressmaker."[20]

Once again, the Orozco humor, dry and acute, was in great form. What is important about this journalistic note is that *Time* considered Orozco a leading voice for Latin America and that the artist stated a clear anti-Eurocentric position.

When Orozco died on September 7, 1949 of heart failure, his obituary was carried in the major papers and art magazines. The *New York Herald Tribune* described him thus: "Concerned all this life with the struggle between man and the machine, José Clemente Orozco found in the broad dimensions of murals the emotional outlet that other men find in speech. He felt that his paintings expressed his deep conviction of the need for social revolution, and that they needed no explanation." The obituary cited his important work in the United States at Pomona, Dartmouth, and New York. It also made a point of mentioning his lack of fame when compared with Rivera, stating that this was due to Orozco's avoidance of fiery debate.[21] In its obituary, *Art News* spoke of Orozco as "one of the founders of the modern Mexican school of fresco and mural painting. . . . Through his forceful and monumental frescoes in government and university build-ings in Mexico and also in the U.S., his influence made its mark in the thirties on the social-conscious paintings here before it attained international proportions."[22] On his death, Orozco was remembered by those sectors of the culture to which in life he had been both attracted and repelled.

Conclusion

In this study of Orozco's New York years, his work has been interpreted not just in the light of formal issues but also within a cultural and sociopolitical context. These years were significant for Orozco; in New York City he produced two important murals, as well as a substantial body of easel and graphic work. While in Gringoland, New York City in particular, Orozco encountered modernity in all its contradictions. It was in Gringoland where Orozco most experimented with his art and where his artistic vision started to crystallize into what I would call a pessimistic view of history, a pessimism different from the less historically grounded view evident in earlier works such as *The House of Tears* series. This historical pessimism was always critical, never nostalgic for a past that never existed nor reactionary regarding an ever-devastating present. Orozco was a political artist—one who functioned in a real and historical world and responded to its political and social dilemmas with his own philosophical insights, weaknesses, and strengths. Ultimately, Orozco's iconoclastic politics were grounded, perhaps even buried, in his anarchist background. With shape and color, he painted what Federico García Lorca expressed in words in the poems of *Poet in New York*: troubled visions of reality yearning for redemption.

Chapter 1

1. Jean Meyer, *La Cristiada: La guerra de los cristeros, vol. 1* (México, D.F.: Siglo XXI, 1973–74), 9–20. This and all translations from the Spanish are by the author. The Cristero War (1926–29) originally started as a conflict between the Roman Catholic hierarchy and the government of Alvaro Obregón. The clash between these two institutions centered on Article 130 of the Revolutionary Constitution of 1922, which, among other things, restricted the freedom of movement of members of the Roman Catholic Church and the practice of their faith. The struggle evolved into a civil war, where the brunt of the fighting was borne by the peasant believers, who had in the 1910s supported Zapata and Villa. With a few exceptions, the institutional church was hostile to the Mexican Revolution, and upper- and middle-class Catholics played counterrevolutionary roles in relation to it.

John M. Hart, *Anarchism, & The Mexican Working Class, 1860–1931,* 2nd ed. (Austin: University of Texas Press, 1987), 156–75. In this seminal work, the most thorough on Mexican anarchism in either Spanish or English, Hart presents the origins and developments of the movement. He discusses the creation of the Casa del Obrero Mundial (September 22, 1912), its support of the Constitutionalist forces within the revolution (Carranza and Obregón), and the evolution of the Casa into the Confederación General de Trabajadores, founded on February 22, 1921. Through Dr. Atl, Orozco came into contact with the Casa's brand of anarcho-syndicalism. This is Orozco's only known political association. The anarchists of the Casa were generally opposed to the religious views of Zapata, Villa, and their followers.

2. Lucrecia Orozco de Herrero, typed response to questionnaire by author, 5 September 1995. "I was born on November 13, 1927, so that on the 11 of December I was less than a month old. In fact, my father waited only for my birth in order to depart for the United States. He left for the United States by train, on the 11 of December, 1927."

3. José Clemente Orozco, *Autobiografía*, 3rd ed. (México, D.F.: Ediciones Era, S.A., 1984), 47–58. Chapter 6 begins on page 47 and ends on page 52; chapter 7 starts on page 53 and concludes on page 58.

4. Orozco, *Autobiografía*, 53.

5. David Alfaro Siqueiros, *Me llamaban el Coronelazo*, 3rd ed. (México, D.F.: Editorial Grijalbo, S.A., 1987), 134–35.

6. Orozco, *Autobiografía*, 53–56, 57–58.

7. Fausto Ramírez, "Artistas e Iniciados en la Obra Mural de Orozco," in *Orozco: Una Relectura*, ed. Xavier Moyssén (México, D.F.: Universidad Nacional Autónoma de México, 1983), 95–97. Ramírez interprets this mural as an allegory of creation, where the Eternal-Masculine (creative spirit, intellectual essence, fire) and the Eternal-Feminine (the soul, passive principle, water) are brought forth by the hands of God. The title itself means knowledge acquired not through the physical eyes but by an inner vision. When and how did Orozco encounter theosophic ideas? According to Ramírez, he did so possibly through his friendship with the poet José Juan Tablada and through his reading of Amado Nervo and José Vasconcelos.

8. Renato González Mello, *Orozco, ¿Pintor Revolucionario?* (México, D.F.: Universidad Nacional Autónoma de México, Instituto de Investigaciones Estéticas, 1995), 26–32. González Mello states that Orozco did not begin to depict scenes of the revolution in his work until 1923. His known easel pictures and watercolors prior to this date are part of *La casa del llanto* series (brothel subjects). Alma Reed and Orozco backdated most of the work of the 1920s—at issue was Orozco's competition with Rivera and having depicted certain subjects first. Either Orozco himself or Anita Brenner brought the unfinished canvases to the United States, where they were completed by 1928.

9. José Vasconcelos, *La flama: Los de arriba en la Revolución* (México, D.F.: Compañia Editorial Continental, S.A., 1959), 293. José Vasconcelos was one of the leading intellectual voices of the Mexican Revolution between the years 1921 and 1923. He had been rector of the National University in

Mexico City under Huerta and Carranza. General Obregón
appointed him secretary of public education, a post he
held until early 1924. In 1929, he ran for the presidency
of Mexico—it is generally believed that the election was
stolen from him by Pascual Ortiz Rubio, the candidate
supported by President Calles. After this incident, Vasconcelos's political career and intellectual integrity went
downhill; he became quite a reactionary, a supporter of
Franco in Spain as well as military dictators throughout
the Americas. Orozco admired Vasconcelos early on and
after he lost political power, yet they did not share the
same political orientation.

10. Octavio Paz, "Re/Visions: Mural Painting" in *Essays on
Mexican Art*, trans. Helen Lane (New York: Harcourt Brace
& Company, 1993), 166.

11. David Craven, *Diego Rivera As Epic Modernist* (New York:
G. K. Hall & Co., 1997), 62.

12. Raquel Tibol, conversation with author, 22 June 1995,
México, D.F. Tibol, a leading art critic, was Rivera's secretary
(1953–54) and Siqueiros's archivist and official biographer
(1955–60). Tibol states that Siqueiros told her that after
they were fired from the Preparatoria, he went to Guadalajara
to assist Amado de la Cueva with a mural he was painting
at the university there. He also recalled that Fernando Leal,
Jean Charlot, and Orozco returned (temporarily) to the
execution of easel pictures. In 1934, the government of
President Lazaro Cárdenas, as part of its progressive
agenda, renewed the commission of murals.

13. Orozco, *Autobiografía*, 85. "Finding Mexico not very
propitious in 1927, I resolved to go to New York."

14. Ibid., 41–45. Proof of his activism are the covers he drew
for *La Vanguardia* on May 10 and 14, 1915 (see fig. 6).

15. Hart, *Anarchism*, 173–74. "The Tampico petroleum strike
quickly deepened with the dispatch of troops to the scene
by President Calles, 'to protect' company property. The
soldiers were involved in shooting incidents and the strikers
retaliated with sabotage. One scholar has observed that
troops were used largely because it was a CGT syndicate
on strike."

16. Ibid., 174–76. Hart states that after the 1927 strike, the
government continued to harass and persecute the CGT.
By 1929, when faced with the CROM's total cooperation
with the government, it lost its sense of direction. By July
1931, the CGT had disbanded.

17. Jean Meyer, *Historia de los cristianos en América Latina,* Siglos XIX y XX, 2nd ed. (México, D. F.: Editorial Vuelta, S.A. De C.V., 1991), 231–33. Meyer states that the conflict started at an institutional level. The government wanted the church to keep its social opinions to itself, the church wanted the government to remove the anti-Catholic articles of the recent constitution. The Vatican, ever the survivor, wanted to continue negotiations. The government had enough conflicts to deal with. Both institutions were surprised at the outbreak of war. Most of the cristero forces were comprised of former followers of Zapata and Villa.

18. Ibid., 236. Jalisco, Colima, and Nayarit were briefly cristero territories. Mexico City, its surrounding areas, and states like Chiapas and Tabasco were staunchly anti-Catholic.

19. Ibid., 240–41. The lay leaders of the troops went into exile either to the United States or France. The troops, as well as the priests at the grassroots level, were betrayed. The best journalistic treatment in English of this subject remains Graham Greene's *The Lawless Roads* (1939) and his fictional treatment of the same subject in *The Power and the Glory* (1940).

20. Antonio Luna Arroyo, conversation with author, 28 June 1995, Guadalajara, Jalisco. Luna Arroyo was a friend and collector of both Orozco and Francisco Goitia. He recalls Orozco's using the phrase *"pinche pais"* whenever he referred to Mexico in 1927 and his decision to leave it.

21. Alfredo Orozco Valladares, conversation with author, 1 July 1995, Cuautla, Morelos. Alfredo Orozco Valladares is the artist's second child. A retired architect, he lives in the small town of Cuautla, some three hours from Mexico City. Orozco Valladares recalls his father telling him (over and over and throughout the years) the story of the sale of the easel paintings *Combate* and *Soldaderas. Combate* is currently in the collection of the Carillo Gil Museum, while *Soldaderas* belongs to the Museum of Modern Art in Mexico City.

22. Ibid.

Chapter 2

1. José Clemente Orozco, letter to Margarita Valladares, 23 December 1927. Collection of Alfredo Orozco Valladares, Cuautla, Morelos, México.

2. Ann Douglas, *Terrible Honesty, Mongrel Manhattan in the 1920s* (New York: Farrar, Strauss and Giroux, 1955), 3.

3. Ibid., 8.

4. "Diego Rivera Exhibition," *Art News*, 15 (October 14, 1916): 3; *Sun*, 23 October 1926, 5. Organized by the Mexican caricaturist Marius de Zayas, the 1916 exhibit was held at the Modern Gallery. Zayas had lived in New York since 1907, earning his living as a caricaturist for the *World*. He would become a collaborator of Alfred Stieglitz as well as an exponent of modernism in the United States.

5. The best discussion of this fashionable interest in Mexican culture is to be found in Helen Delpar, *The Enormous Vogue of Things Mexican* (University of Alabama Press, 1992). Orozco's reservations regarding this "vogue" is found in his correspondence with Charlot and Margarita, and in the *Autobiografía*. His reservations were based on his distrust of fashion and what he considered to be the bad taste of tourists.

6. José Clemente Orozco, *El artista en Nueva York (Cartas a Jean Charlot y textos inéditos, 1925–29)*, (México, D.F.: Siglo XXI, 1971), 33–36. Letter to Jean Charlot, 21 December 1927.

7. Ibid. Walter Pach was an art critic and painter who had been one of the organizers of the 1913 Armory Show. In 1929, Pach published *Ananias, or the False Artist*, a book that contains favorable comments on Orozco, although both Picasso and Rivera receive the greatest praise. The most complete discussion of Pach's art criticism is in Sandra S. Phillips, "The Art Criticism of Walter Pach," *The Art Bulletin*, no. 1, vol. LXV (March 1983): 106–22.

8. Orozco, *El artista en Nueva York*, 38. Letter to Jean Charlot, 3 January 1928.

9. Ibid., 39–41. Letter to Jean Charlot, 4 January 1928.

10. Anita Brenner, letter to Jean Charlot, 16 January 1947, Charlot Papers, Thomas Hale Hamilton Library, University of Hawaii, Honolulu.

11. Anita Brenner, "A Mexican Rebel," *The Arts*, no. 4, vol. XII (October 1927): 201–9.

12. José Clemente Orozco, *Cartas a Margarita* (México, D.F.: Ediciones Era, S.A., 1987), 117. Letter to Margarita Valladares, 30 June 1928.

13. Ibid., 121–22. Letter to Margarita Valladares, 2 August 1928.

14. Antoinette May, *Passionate Pilgrim: The Extraordinary Life of Alma Reed* (New York: Marlowe & Company, 1994), 4, 13. This is the only biography of Reed, one filled with inconsistencies and errors and too reliant on Reed's own 1956 biography of Orozco. Yet the basic facts of her early life are accurate.

15. Ibid., 72.

16. Ibid., 212.

17. The Art Center, "Mexican Art," January 19–February 14, 1928, 65 East 56th Street, New York City. Exhibition announcement, Orozco Papers, Visual Art Archives, O.A.S., Washington, D.C.

18. Orozco, *El artista en Nueva York*, 54. Letter to Jean Charlot, 23 February 1928.

19. Ibid., 102. Letter to Jean Charlot, 10 September 1928.

20. Orozco, *Cartas a Margarita*, 128. Letter to Margarita Valladares, 21 September 1928. Orozco does not note the painting's title, only that Sikelianos paid him $300 by check.

21. Orozco, *Autobiografía*, 88.

22. Ibid., 91.

23. José Vasconcelos (1881–1959), politician and philosopher, had the Greek classics translated into Spanish and published in affordable editions. He identified himself with Ulysses, entitling a volume of his autobiography *Ulíses criollo* (1935). Alfonso Reyes (1889–1959), poet and essayist, attempted a synthetic reading of the pre-Cortesian past with the heroic proportions of Greek myths. This concern is reflected in his *Visión de anáhuac* (1917) and *Ifigenia cruel* (1924). Reyes and Orozco were friendly until the painter's death in 1949.

24. Orozco, *Cartas a Margarita*, 130. Letter to Margarita Valladares, 28 September 1928.

25. Alma Reed, letter to José Clemente Orozco, 26 September 1928. Collection of Lucrecia Orozco Valladares, Guadalajara, Jalisco, México.

26. Galleries of Marie Sterner, "Mexico in Revolution," October 10–22, 9 East 57th Street, New York City. Exhibition announcement, Orozco Papers, Visual Art Archives, O.A.S., Washington, D.C.

27. Orozco, *El artista en Nueva York*, 119. Letter to Jean Charlot, 8 October 1928.

28. Orozco, *Cartas a Margarita*, 134. Letter to Margarita Valladares, 2 October 1928.

29. Galleries of Marie Sterner, sales records, Sterner papers, Archives of American Art, Washington, D.C. Not a single critical notice for the exhibition appeared in either the newspapers or the art magazines. According to the records, nothing was sold.

30. Orozco, *Cartas a Margarita*, 138. Letter to Margarita Valladares, 20 October 1928.

31. Ibid., 141. Letter to Margarita Valladares, 16 November 1928.

32. Ibid., 141, 144. Letters to Margarita Valladares, 16 November, and 6 December, 1928.

33. Orozco, *El artista en Nueva York*. See letters of 23 February 1928 (55), 20 March 1928 (63), and 25 September 1928 (117).

34. Ibid., 63. Letter to Jean Charlot, 20 March 1928.

35. Ibid., 41. Letter to Jean Charlot, 4 January 1928.

36. Orozco, *Cartas a Margarita*, 147. Letter to Margarita Valladares, 25 January 1929. Orozco complains that he has been paid for only one of the lithographs. He does give the titles of the lithographs. The Downtown Gallery records of this period are incomplete.

37. The Downtown Gallery, "José Orozco: Paintings of New York City," March 26–April 15, 1929, 113 West 13th Street, New York City. Exhibition announcement, Orozco papers, Visual Art Archives, O.A.S., Washington, D.C.

38. Orozco, *El artista en Nueva York*, 129. Letter to Jean Charlot, 19 February 1929.

39. Sotheby's, "Important Latin American Paintings, Drawings and Sculpture," May 28–29, 1985, 1334 York Avenue, New York, New York. Auction catalog, plate 30. Mrs. John D. Rockefeller sold the work through Halpert after World War II. The work was acquired by Enid F. Goldsmith, who owned other works by Orozco. The Goldsmith estate was auctioned by Sotheby's in May 1985.

40. José Clemente Orozco, "New World, New Races, and New Art." *Creative Art*, vol. 4, no. 1 (January 1929): suppl. 44–46.

41. Orozco, *Cartas a Margarita*, 150. Letter to Margarita Valladares, 15 February 1929. The exhibition opened on February 13 and ran for two weeks. George Biddle (1885–1973) befriended Orozco through Walter Pach and later painted Orozco's portrait, which according to Orozco made him look like Lincoln (Orozco, *El artista en Nueva York*, 129. Letter to Jean Charlot, 1 February 1929). Biddle recalled his friendship with Orozco in his 1939 autobiography *An American Artist's Story*.

42. Ibid., 151. Letter to Margarita Valladares, 24 February 1929. The Modotti photographs of the Preparatoria murals would be used to illustrate Reed's 1932 monograph on Orozco.

43. José Clemente Orozco, letter to Margarita Valladares, 3 April 1929. Thomas Hart Benton (1889–1975) met Orozco in 1929 and invited him to exhibit at the Art Student's League in April of that year. They both painted murals at the New School for Social Research in 1930–31. In his 1937 autobiography, *An Artist in America*, Benton does not mention Orozco. The Benton correspondence of this period also does not mention Orozco.

44. Will Barnet, telephone interview with author, 17 October 1995.

45. Orozco, *Cartas a Margarita*, 156. Letter to Margarita Valladares, 18 April 1929.

46. Orozco, *El artista en Nueva York*, 57. Letter to Jean Charlot, 23 February 1928.

47. Orozco, *Cartas a Margarita*, 161. Letter to Margarita Valladares, 16 June 1929.

48. Chicago Arts Club, "Drawings and Paintings by José Clemente Orozco," June 15–29, 1928, Chicago, Illinois. Exhibition announcement, Orozco papers, Visual Art Archives, O.A.S., Washington, D.C. This announcement and Orozco's mention in the letter to his wife are the only remaining records of this exhibition. There is no record of it among the Arts Club papers, and there is no mention of the exhibition in the local press.

49. Orozco, *Cartas a Margarita*, 161. Letter to Margarita Valladares, 16 June 1929.

50. Ibid.

51. Margarita Valladares, letter to author, 3 September 1992. Orozco stayed with his family in Mexico City from late June through September 3, 1929.

52. Ibid. "My husband and Alma Reed came to an agreement regarding the promotion of his work, before he returned to Mexico in the summer of 1929. She was going to be his representative, and she was thinking of opening a gallery dedicated to his work."

53. Raquel Tibol, conversation with author, 22 June 1995, México, D.F. Tibol remembers that after Reed's death all of her papers disappeared. She recalls that Siqueiros was indignant that the Reed papers did not end up in the archives of the Instituto Nacional de Bellas Artes.

54. Orozco, *Cartas a Margarita*, 162. Letter to Margarita Valladares, 8 September 1929.

55. Ibid., 167. Letter to Margarita Valladares, 16 October 1929.

56. Ibid., 168. Letter to Margarita Valladares, 16 October 1929. Orozco adds that spending time with Rivas Mercado is a waste, since he has many other things that need doing.

57. Antonieta Rivas Mercado, letter to Manuel Rodríguez Lozano, 20 October 1929. Manuel Rodríguez Lozano papers, Archives del Instituto Nacional de Bellas Artes, México D.F. The Abraham referred to is Abraham Angel (1905–1924), a painter and former student/lover of Rodríguez Lozano's who had died very young. The Julio referred to is Julio Castellanos 1905–1947), also a former student of Rodríguez Lozano's and an extraordinary easel painter of genre scenes. Antonieta Rivas Mercado committed suicide by shooting herself in Notre Dame Cathedral in 1931. At the time, she was living in Paris with Vasconcelos.

58. Thomas Hart Benton, *An American in Art* (Lawrence: University of Kansas Press, 1969), 61. Benton mentions Orozco several times in his 1969 autobiography, while there is no mention of him in the earlier *An Artist in America* of 1937.

59. Orozco, *Autobiografía*, 96–97.

60. Antoinette May makes such a claim in her Reed biography of 1994. Will Barnet told me that, although he had no proof, he believed that Orozco and Reed were lovers (telephone interview with author, 17 October 1995). The verdict here is still out. Certainly Orozco was by no means a saint; in the last decade of his life he had an affair with the Mexican choreographer Nellie Campobello.

61. Churchill Lathrop, conversation with author, 24 October 1991, Montclair, New Jersey. Lathrop was professor of art history at Dartmouth College 1928–66. He recalls visiting the Delphic Studios in the early 1930s and always finding a quasi-permanent display of Orozco paintings, drawings, and gouaches.

62. Benton, *An American in Art*, 69. Benton mentions the other artists as showing and selling through the Delphic Studios. Fidelio Ponce (1892–1949) was a Cuban expressionist painter whose work was championed by Alfred H. Barr Jr., director of The Museum of Modern Art in New York. Reed exhibited Ponce's work in 1937.

63. In all of my conversations with two of Orozco's children, Alfredo and Lucrecia, as well as in questionnaires to them, they agree on the decrease of Orozco's prices while in the United States. They received this information from their father and also from their mother.

64. According to the acquisition records of the Carillo Gil Museum, Dr. Carillo Gil acquired eleven easel works by Orozco, ranging in dates from 1929 through 1930, for no more than $7,000.

65. Churchill Lathrop, conversation with author, 24 October 1991. Lathrop remembered Reed as "a mature yet beautiful woman who could be aggressive"; he thought her knowledge of art was limited. Will Barnet, letter to author, 16 April 1996. Barnet described Reed as "attractive, someone who could be an aggressive champion for Orozco. Yet she lacked the knowledge and know-how of an Edith Halpert."

66. Orozco, *Cartas a Margarita*, 241. Letter to Margarita Valladares, 26 May 1931.

67. Ibid., 241. Rivera would be the second artist (after Matisse) to have a retrospective at The Museum of Modern Art in New York.

68. José Clemente Orozco, letter to Margarita Valladares, 16 November 1932.

69. Alma Reed, *Orozco* (New York: Oxford University, 1956), 137.

70. Alfredo Orozco Valladares, conversation with author, 1 July 1995, Cuautla, Morelos, México.

71. Orozco, *Cartas a Margarita*, 241. Letter to Margarita Valladares, 26 May 1931. In this letter, Orozco complains that Reed will take 50 percent of the sales to Stephen C. Clark. He also mentions Reed's lack of records for recent sales and his not knowing what is owed to him. This continues with regularity throughout the correspondence with Margarita through 1934.

72. An example of this are the drawings for the *México en Revolución* series. Reed's book alleges that they are based on sketches of 1913 to 1917, a period when Orozco was painting the brothel pictures of the *Casa del llanto* series. These drawings in reality were executed some nine or ten years later. The sketches upon which they are supposedly based are non-existent, while all other preparatory sketches by Orozco exist.

73. "Recent Art Books," *Art Digest*, (7 January 1933): 8.

74. Orozco, *Cartas a Margarita*, 278. Letter to Margarita Valladares, 28 April 1934. Orozco states that the book has been selling since its publication at both the Delphic Studios and the Weyhe Gallery and that Misrachi has bought a number of them to sell in his bookstore in Mexico City.

75. Margarita Valladares de Orozco, letter to author, 3 September 1992. According to Orozco's widow, when he returned to Mexico in 1934, his connections with the Delphic Studios and its director were over. Reed kept an inventory of Orozco's work that she continued to exhibit and sell, even though, according to this source, the artist did not see a penny from these sales. Until her death in January 1993, Margarita believed that Reed tried to get the artist to leave his family and dedicate himself only to his art. Although Margarita never admitted that an affair between Orozco and Reed happened, she believed Reed wanted to be "more than just the artist's dealer."

76. Orozco, *Cartas a Margarita*, 302. Letter to Margarita Valladares, 25 May 1940.

77. Ibid., 300. Letter to Margarita Valladares, 10 May 1940. It is also important to note that all references to the Delphic Studios in the art magazines cease by January 1940.

78. Reed, *Orozco*, 29, 271, 272–308. The major problems with this biography are Reed's subjectivity and her mythologized account of the artist's life.

79. Orozco, *Autobiografía*, 106.

80. Ibid., 106–8.

81. Ibid., 109.

82. Ibid.

Chapter 3

1. José Clemente Orozco, *Orozco "Explains"* (New York: The Museum of Modern Art, 1940), 9.

2. Reed, *Orozco*, 64.

3. The Carillo Gil registry extends beyond its own collection. In spite of its incompleteness, it is the closest thing to a complete Orozco catalog. Orozco titled the New York and mythological scenes in English (probably with Alma Reed's help); all other subjects he titled in Spanish. The following is the list of easel works by category that I was able to identify:

New York scenes
    1. *Coney Island*, 1928
    2. *The Subway*, 1928
    3. *New York Factory, Williamsburg*, 1928
    4. *Queensborough Bridge*, 1928
    5. *The Elevated*, 1928 (vertical version)
    6. *The Third Avenue Elevated*, 1928 (horizontal)
    7. *Eighth Avenue*, 1928
    8. *Fourteenth Street, Manhattan*, 1928

9. *Subway Post*, 1929
10. *Street Corner (Manhattan)*, 1929
11. *The City*, 1930
12. *World's Highest Structure*, 1930
13. *Construction*, 1930
14. *The Curb*, 1930
15. *The Dead*, 1931
16. *Successful People*, 1931
17. *Winter*, 1932
18. *Three Heads*, 1932
19. *Bank Holiday*, 1932–33

Mexican scenes
20. *Mujer con maguey*, 1928
21. *Casa Mexicana*, 1929
22. *Casa de Piedra*, 1929
23. *Soldado herido*, 1930
24. *La paz*, 1930
25. *Zapatistas*, 1931
26. *La trinchera* (or *Barricade*), 1931
27. *El cementerio*, 1931
28. *Pancho Villa*, 1931
29. *Maguey*, 1932
30. *Pueblo Mexicano*, 1932
31. *Paisaje Mexicano*, 1932

Mythological (Greek–inspired) or surreal subjects
32. *The Teacher*, 1929
33. *Broken Glass*, 1929
34. *Vigil*, 1929
35. *Embrace*, 1929
36. *Fallen Columns*, 1930
37. *Drama*, 1930
38. *The Mirror*, 1930
39. *Aquella noche*, 1930

Portraits
40. *Eva Sikelianos*, 1928
41. *Autorretrato*, 1928 (lost)
42. *Julia Peterkin*, 1929
43. *Alma Reed*, 1929 (destroyed by Orozco)
44. *Patsy Sullivan*, 1930 (Reed's niece; portrait started in San Francisco and finished in New York, lost) Based on conversations with two of the Orozco children (Alfredo and Lucrecia), it seems that there were some ten to twelve easel paintings that he began in New York but never completed. These were all probably small oils on canvas.

4. Reed, *Orozco*, 123.

5. Alfredo Orozco Valladares, conversation with author, 1 July 1995, Cuautla, Morelos, México.

6. José Clemente Orozco, Notebook 1, unpaginated. Collection of Alfredo Orozco Valladares, Cuautla, Morelos, México. For the sake of clarity, I will refer to Orozco's notebooks in the following manner: Notebook 1 (1931), Notebook 2 (1931–32), Notebook 3 (1932), Notebook 4 (1933), Notebook 5 (1934), Notebook 6 (1934). This information comes out of one of six notebooks kept by Orozco from 1931 through 1934. They are dated irregularly with the years 1931–32, 1933, and 1934, and contain all sorts of notes, quick sketches, and geometric diagrams.

7. Orozco, Notebook 2, unpaginated.

8. There are seals on the back of all six notebooks, also on the stretchers of paintings, such as *Pancho Villa* and *Winter*. Orozco mentions the store in a number of letters to Margarita from 1929 and 1930.

9. Orozco, *Autobiografía*, 85, 87.

10. Ibid., 54.

11. Luis Cardoza y Aragón, letter to author, 6 October 1991. Luis Cardoza y Aragón (1904–1992) wrote extensively on Orozco (*La nube y el reloj*, 1940; *Orozco*, 1959) and was friendly with him until his death. He also met García Lorca in both Cuba and Spain before the outbreak of the civil war. According to Cardoza y Aragón, García Maroto introduced García Lorca to Orozco while both were in New York. Years later, Orozco recalled to Cardoza y Aragón that he had met the poet a number of times for lunch, to chat and to visit Harlem. There is no mention of García Lorca in any of the Orozco correspondence; the artist probably considered the poet as someone very young and not fully formed as a writer, definitely not important enough to mention in his letters.

12. Federico García Lorca, *Poet in New York*, translated by Greg Simon and Steven F. White (New York: The Noonday Press, 1988), 53–55.

13. The best discussion of the paintings of the Fourteenth Street School is to be found in Ellen Wiley Todd, *The "New Woman" Revised: Painting and Gender Politics on Fourteenth Street* (University of California Press, 1993). Todd mentions briefly Orozco's painting *Fourteenth Street, Manhattan* as a negative statement of both urban life and womanhood.

14. Gail Stavitsky, *Reordering Reality: Precisionism in America* (New York: The Montclair Art Museum and Harry N. Abrams, Inc., 1994), 28–29.

15. Federico García Lorca, letter to Luis Cardoza y Aragón, sent from Havana, Cuba, 6 April 1930.

16. Quoted in Reed, *Orozco*, 28.

17. Margaret Brening, "Orozco at the Downtown Gallery," *The New York Post*, 31 March 1929, sec. 1, p. 17, col. 2.

18. Lloyd Goodrich, "In the Galleries," *The Arts*, vol. XVI, no. 6 (February 1930): 423.

19. Orozco, *Autobiografía*, 94–95.

20. By "formal" I am referring to the quotations of pre-Columbian forms in the shapes found in the works of Charlot, Tamayo, and Amero.

21. Orozco, *Autobiografía*, 34.

22. Since the 1940 exhibition *20 Centuries of Mexican Art*, The Museum of Modern Art has had both a six-by-four-inch postcard and a nine-by-twelve-inch color reproduction of *Zapatistas* for sale in its museum store. Since the 1992 *Modern Art of Latin America* exhibition, a six-by-four-inch postcard of *Barricade* has also been available.

23. Gómez Sicre, typed manuscript of Orozco interview, 13 February 1946, 1.

24. Orozco, *Autobiografía*, 45.

25. Orozco, *Cartas a Margarita*, 241. Letter to Margarita Valladares, 20 May 1931.

26. Orozco Valladares, *Orozco, verdad cronológica*, (Guadalajara, 1983), 247. *La trinchera* was reproduced in Reed's 1932 book on Orozco as *Barricade*, a title by which it has been known ever since.

27. Orozco, Notebook 1, 1931, unpaginated.

28. Ibid.

29. Ibid.

30. Hart, *Anarchism*, 126–27.

31. Enrique Krauze, *Francisco Villa, Entre el ángel y el fierro* (México, D.F.: Fondo de Cultura Económica, 1987), 7–11, 92–97, 107, 110–11.

32. The most thorough and the only political discussion of Orozco's *Zapata Entering a Peasant's Hut* is in John Hutton, "If I am to die tomorrow," Roots and Meanings of Orozco's "Zapata Entering a Peasant's Hut," in *The Art Institute of Chicago Museum Studies*, vol. II, no. 1 (Fall 1984): 38–51.

33. Orozco, Notebook 3, unpaginated.

34. As indicated in chapter 2, this exhibition took place at the Galleries of Marie Sterner October 10–22, 1928.

35. Alfredo Orozco Valladares, conversation with author, 1 July 1995, Cuautla, Morelos, México. The artist's son remembers hearing his father mention, years after the fact, that Brenner had brought some of his drawings to the United States before he arrived in December 1927; Orozco feared his work could be destroyed once again by United States Customs agents, as had happened earlier with the *Casa del llanto* series.

36. Ibid. Alfredo Orozco Valladares recalls his father telling him of drawing more "estampas de la revolución" once he was already in New York City.

37. Reed, *Orozco*, 130.

38. Orozco, *Autobiografía*, 42.

39. Ibid., 46.

40. Luis Leal, *Mariano Azuela* (México, D.F.: Fondo de Cultura Económica, 1971), 25–28.

41. Orozco, *El Artista en Nueva York*, 30. Letter to Jean Charlot, 19 February 1929.

42. Mariano Azuela, *The Underdogs*, trans. Enrique Munguía (New York: Brentano's, 1929).

43. Orozco, *El Artista en Nueva York*, 56–57. Letter to Jean Charlot, 23 February 1928.

44. Chronologically, these are the lithographs executed by Orozco while in New York City:

   1. *Vaudeville in Harlem*, 1928
   2. *Bandera*, 1928
   3. *Requiem*, 1928
   4. *Casa arruinada*, 1929
   5. *Retaguardia*, 1929
   6. *Soldados Mexicanos*, 1929
   7. *Revolución*, 1929
   8. *Inditos*, 1929
   9. *Maguey*, 1929
   10. *Paisaje Mexicano*, 1930
   11. *Pueblo Mexicano*, 1930
   12. *Manos entrelazadas*, 1930
   13. *Manos*, 1930
   14. *Aflicción*, 1930
   15. *Franciscano*, 1930
   16. *Embarazada*, 1930
   17. *Cabeza de campesina*, 1930
   18. *Tres generaciones*, 1930
   19. *Negros ahorcados* (or *The American Scene*), 1930

45. Will Barnet, telephone interview with author, 4 April 1996. Barnet recalls printing an image of a "family and another of a peasant woman in profile, both on zinc plates. Alma Reed brought them to me at the League."

46. All of the original studies belong to the artist's older son, Clemente, who resides in both Mexico City and Guadalajara. I saw photographs of these studies in the collection of the artist's second son, Alfredo, when I visited him in Cuautla.

47. Marlene Park, "Lynching and Antilynching: Art and Politics in the 1930s," *Prospects*, vol. 18 (Cambridge: Cambridge University Press, 1993): 329–37.

48. Ibid., 324–25.

49. Luigi Marrozzini and Clemente Orozco V., *Catálogo Completo de la Obra Gráfica de Orozco* (San Juan: Instituto de Cultura Puertorriqueña, Universidad de Puerto Rico, 1970), 48. The principal problem with this catalog is Marrozzini's total reliance on Orozco's oldest son, Clemente, as the single source of information on the prints. According to the *Encyclopedia of the American Left* (University of Illinois Press, 1992), the American Civil Rights Congress was founded in June 1946 and was most active from 1946 to 1953. In the mid-1950s, it was destroyed by the alleged infiltration of the CIA and the pressures of the Cold War.

50. A. Jakira, "As if to Slaughter," *Labor Defender*, no. 5 (June 1930): 126.

51. This is a suite of thirteen aquatints, the subjects of which range from unemployed figures to beggars, prostitutes, and clowns. In both composition and treatment they have qualities similar to Rouault's prints of the early 1920s.

52. Laurence Schmeckebier, "Orozco's Graphic Art," *The Print Collectors Quarterly*, London, vol. 21, no. 2 (April 1934): 194.

53. J. H. Hopkins, *Orozco: A Catalog of his Graphic Work* (Flagstaff: University of Northern Arizona Press, 1967).

Chapter 4

1. Jewell in his *New York Times* review of January 25, 1931, found the murals "with genuine regret disappointing." He added that the panels were "a mêlée of fragments without—from the standpoint of design—any relationship" He obviously missed the point of Dynamic Symmetry. Since this first review, writers as diverse as Justino Fernández, Luis Cardoza y Aragón, MacKinley Helm, and most recently Laurence Hurlburt have found the murals contrived and programmatic.

2. Reed, *Orozco*, 198, 204.

3. Donald L. Miller, *Lewis Mumford: A Life* (Pittsburgh: University of Pittsburgh Press, 1989), 329. According to Miller, Mumford was not only instrumental in the New School commission but also in the commission of the Baker Library at Dartmouth, since Mumford was friendly with both Artemas Packard, chair of the art department there, and Churchill Lathrop, professor of art history. Mumford never quite became a close friend of Orozco; he found the Mexican's shyness difficult to get through. Like Orozco, Mumford had a background in anarchism and, like Orozco, in later life became critical of technology.

4. Benton, *An American in Art*, 62.

5. Quoted in Hurlburt, *Mexican Muralists*, 43.

6. Benton, *An American in Art*, 63.

7. Alvin Johnson, "Notes on the New School Murals," pamphlet of 1943, 2–3.

8. Orozco, "New World, New Races and New Art," 44.

9. Kenneth Frampton, *Modern Architecture: A Critical History* (New York: Oxford University Press, 1980), 85.

10. Ivo Frenzel, "Prophet, Pioneer, Seducer: Friedrich Nietzsche's Influence on Art, Literature and Philosophy in Germany," in Christos M. Joachimides, Norman Rosenthal, and Wieland Schmied, *German Art in the 20th Century Painting and Sculpture 1900–85* (Munich: Prestel Verlag, 1985), 77.

11. Miguel Bueno, "El arte de Diego Rivera atacado por el genial artista C. Orozco," *El Imparcial*, 22 November 1926, 7. Bueno quotes Orozco on Rivera throughout this article.

12. Jean Charlot, *The Mexican Mural Renaissance, 1920–25* (New Haven: Yale University Press, 1962), 77.

13. Ibid., 82.

14. José Vasconcelos, *Pitagoras* in *Obras completas*, vol. 1 (México, D.F.: Fondo de Cultura Económica, 1982–83), 82.

15. José Ortega y Gassett discusses these ideas most clearly in his books *La rebelión de las masas, España invertebrada*, and *El tema de nuestro tiempo*, all written between the end of World War I and 1926.

16. The program of the Delphic Festival or Society has been presented or discussed in a fragmented manner in articles in periodicals such as *The Mentor, The Independent*, and *The Literary Digest*. The only complete version of the program is Angelos Sikelianos, *Plan général du mouvement delphique* (Paris: Les Belles Lettres, 1929), 26–29, 41–44.

17. Orozco, *Autobiografía*, 99–100, 101.

18. Ibid., 102.

19. Ibid., 101–2.

20. Ibid., 103.

21. The best discussion of this search for order is in C. Greene, *Cubism and Its Enemies* (New Haven: Yale University Press,1987).

22. Albert Christ-Janer, *Boardman Robinson* (Chicago: University of Chicago Press, 1946), 53.

23. Justino Fernández, *Orozco forma e idea*, 2nd ed. (México, D.F.: Editorial Porrúa, S.A., 1975), 57, 59.

24. Luis Cardoza y Aragón, *Orozco* (México, D.F.: Fondo de Cultura Económica, 1983), 123, 54.

25. MacKinley Helm, *Man of Fire: J. C. Orozco* (New York: Harcourt, Brace and Company, 1953), 51, 53.

26. Helen Appleton Reade, "Review," *Brooklyn Eagle,* 1 February 1931, 17.

27. Goodrich, "The Murals of The New School," 403, 444.

28. Fairfield Porter, "Murals for Workers," *Arise* (vol. I, no. 4, 1935).

29. Ibid.

30. Orozco, *Autobiografía,* 99.

31. Reed, *Orozco,* 207.

32. Ibid., 209.

33. The best discussion of the international liberalism of the New School is in William B. Scott, *New School: A History of The New School for Social Research* (New York: Harcourt, Brace and Company, 1986). A focus on the "University in Exile" and the fellow-traveler aspect of the school during the war is to be found in Claus Dieter Krohn, *Wissenschaft im exil* (Munich: Campus Verlag, 1987).

34. Reed, *Orozco,* 207.

35. Porter, "Murals for Workers."

36. Edward Alden Jewell, "Review," *The New York Times,* 25 January 1931, sec. 5, 11.

37. The best discussion of this failed rebellion is in Paul Avrich, *Kronstadt 1921* (Princeton University Press, 1970). The rebellion at Kronstadt was led by communists, socialists, and anarchists.

38. The most thorough discussion of Carrillo Puerto and the Yucatecan agrarian reform is in Francisco J. Paoli Bolio and Enrique Montalvo, *El socialismo olvidado de Yucatán* (México: Fondo de Cultura Económica, 1977).

39. Reed, *Orozco,* 239–40.

40. Albert Boime, *The Academy and French Painting in the Nineteenth Century* (New Haven: Yale University Press, 1971), 26, fig. 7.

41. Charlot, *The Mexican Mural Renaissance,* 6.

42. Shifra M. Goldman, *Contemporary Mexican Painting in a Time of Change* (Austin: University of Texas Press, 1981), 14.

43. *The New Masses* ignored the New School murals by Orozco. We must keep in mind that Gandhi as a non-violent nationalist was not a favorite of the Communists. In 1932, the magazine would revile Rivera for taking on a commission at Rockefeller Center.

44. "New School Keeps Red Mural Hidden," *New York Times,* 22 May 1953, sec. 1. The curtain was removed in 1956.

45. Ibid.

46. Goldman, *Contemporary Mexican Painting,* 9.

Chapter 5

1. Laurance Hurlburt, *The Mexican Muralists in the United States* (Albuquerque: University of New Mexico Press, 1989), 85.

2. José Clemente Orozco, letter to Margarita Valladares, 7 June 1934.

3. Francisco Reyes Palma, "La LEAR y su revista de frente cultural," in *FRENTE a FRENTE 1934–1938, Edición facsimilar* (México, D.F.: Centro de Estudios del Movimiento Obrero y Socialista, A.C., 1994), 5. The government of President Lazaro Cárdenas (1934–40) actively supported the Spanish Republic in its struggle against fascism. After the fascist victory in Spain in 1939, Mexico welcomed many Spanish refugees.

4. Ibid., no. 3 (May 1935), 8.

5. Ibid., no. 2 (April 1936), 19.

6. Matthew Baigell and Julia Williams, *Artists against War and Fascism. Papers of the First American Artists Congress* (New Brunswick: Rutgers University Press, 1986), 5–12.

7. Ibid., 30–32.

8. Ibid., 203.

9. Ibid., 204, 206.

10. Ibid., 208–12.

11. Orozco published *ROJO* in Guadalajara, once a month, from March through June 1936. The first issue dates from March 1; the last from June 7. The Orozco archives at the Museo-Taller in Guadalajara contain a complete set. Justino Fernández's *Textos de Orozco* contains two texts originally published in *ROJO.*

12. Reyes Palma, *FRENTE a FRENTE 1934–1938*, 7.

13. Helm, *Man of Fire*, 83.

14. Orozco, *Autobiografía*, 54.

15. Ibid., 55.

16. The Museum of Modern Art, *Diego Rivera* (New York: W. W. Norton & Company, Inc., 1931). The catalog contains an introduction by Frances Flynn Paine, technical notes on fresco painting by Jere Abbott, a checklist of 146 works, and seventy-one black-and-white illustrations.

17. Alice Goldfarb Marquis, *Alfred H. Barr, Jr., Missionary for the Modern* (Chicago: Contemporary Books, 1989), 51.

18. Laurance Hurlburt, "Diego Rivera (1886–1957): A Chronology of His Art, Life and Times," in the Detroit Institute of Art, *Diego Rivera: A Retrospective* (New York: W. W. Norton & Company, 1986), 30–53.

19. Alfred H. Barr, Jr., "Russian Diary," in Alfred H. Barr, Jr., *Defining Modern Art: Selected Writings of Alfred H. Barr, Jr.* (New York: Harry N. Abrams, Inc., 1986), 134.

20. Irene Herner de Larrea, *Diego Rivera: Paradise Lost at Rockefeller Center* (México, D.F.: Edicupes, S.A. De C.V., 1987), 41.

21. Stanton L. Catlin, "Mural Census," in the Detroit Institute of Art, *Diego Rivera: A Retrospective* (New York: W. W. Norton & Company, 1986), 295–96.

22. Orozco, *Cartas a Margarita*, 300. Letter to Margarita Valladares, 10 May 1940.

23. Ibid., 301. Letter to Margarita Valladares, 21 May 1940.

24. Ibid., 302. Letter to Margarita Valladares, 25 May 1940.

25. José Clemente Orozco, letter to Margarita Valladares, 29 May 1940.

26. Orozco, *Cartas a Margarita*, 305–06. Letter to Margarita Valladares, 10 June 1940.

27. Ibid., 309. Letter to Margarita Valladares, 24 June 1940.

28. Stanton L. Catlin, interview with Lewis Rubinstein, Poughkeepsie, New York, 4 February 1993. Stanton L. Catlin papers, Syracuse, New York, n.p. Shortly before his death, Catlin promised me a copy of this unpublished interview. After his death, a copy was made available to me by his former student Maria Balderrama.

29. Jacob Lawrence, telephone interview with author, 25 March 1993.

30. Bernarda Bryson Shahn, telephone interview with author, 25 March 1993.

31. Stanton L. Catlin, interview with Lewis Rubinstein, Poughkeepsie, New York, 4 February 1993.

32. The Museum of Modern Art, *Orozco "Explains,"* 3.

33. Stanton L. Catlin, interview with Lewis Rubinstein, Poughkeepsie, New York, 4 February 1993.

34. The Museum of Modern Art, *Orozco "Explains,"* 7.

35. Stanton L. Catlin, interview with Lewis Rubinstein, Poughkeepsie, New York, 4 February 1993.

36. Orozco, *Cartas a Margarita*, 310. Letter to Margarita Valladares, 5 July 1940.

37. José Clemente Orozco, letter to Margarita Valladares, 7 July 1940.

38. The Museum of Modern Art, *Orozco "Explains,"* 3.

39. Ibid., 4.

40. Ibid.

41. Ibid., 6.

42. Ibid., 7.

43. Margarita Valladares, letter to author, 3 September 1992. Ricardo Flores Magón (1874–1922) was a journalist and anarchist revolutionary who started his career in opposition to the regime of Porfirio Díaz. He lived in exile in the United States from 1904 on. He was arrested in 1918 under the Espionage Act of 1917, since as an anarchist he opposed World War I. He died in Leavenworth penitentiary in obscure circumstances. He left behind hundreds of articles, which were anthologized after his death. An excellent biography of Flores Magón is Ward S. Albro, *Always a Rebel: Ricardo Flores Magón and the Mexican Revolution* (Austin: University of Texas Press, 1992).

44. José Riera, "Introducción," in Riera, ed., *Antología anarquista* (México, D.F.: Ediciones El Caballito, 1980), 7–8.

45. Cardoza y Aragón, *Orozco*, 231–43. José Gómez Sicre, interview with author, 7 February 1991. Gómez Sicre (1916–91), art critic and chief of the Visual Arts Section at the Organization of American States (1949–83), remembers his conversations with the artist during World War II: "He saw the war as a catastrophe of enormous proportion, fascism had to be defeated, but he [Orozco] was fearful of what would come after. He saw *Catarsis* and *Dive Bomber and Tank* as his two visual statements regarding fascism and war."

46. Fernández, *Orozco forma e idea*, 102, 106.

47. Cardoza y Aragón, *Orozco*, 53.

48. Helm, *Man of Fire*, 83–84.

49. Ibid., 84–85.

50. Riva Castleman, *Art of the Forties* (New York: The Museum of Modern Art and Harry N. Abrams, Inc., 1991), 40.

51. Ibid., 140.

52. Alfred H. Barr, Jr., *What Is Modern Painting?* (New York: The Museum of Modern Art, 1946), 10.

53. "Muralist Gives Explanation of 'Dive Bomber,'" *New York Herald Tribune*, 4 July 1940.

54. "Orozco Completes Fresco at Museum," *New York Times*, 4 July 1940, sec. 1.

55. Luis Cardoza y Aragón, letter to author, 7 October 1991: "Orozco signed the international petition for peace in 1948 and I believe also before his death. In Mexico Rivera and Siqueiros signed, as well as other important intellectuals." Sponsored by the Mexican Communist Party, this petition also had the signatures of poet Carlos Pellicer and novelist José Revueltas. Similar petitions were circulated in Chile, Argentina, and Cuba.

Epilogue

1. Lucrecia Orozco de Herrero, interview with author, 27 June 1995, Guadalajara, Jalisco, México.

2. Orozco, *Cartas a Margarita*, 311. Letter to Margarita Valladares, 23 September 1945. After interviewing by telephone Jorge Martínez (b. 1919), who was Orozco's assistant during the execution of the 1938–39 Guadalajara murals, I have shed further light on the Reed-Orozco relationship. Martínez assured me that Reed visited Orozco in Guadalajara in 1938–39 and stayed with him while the family was in Mexico City. Martínez saw them hold hands and go out to dinner together in what he termed a level of intimacy. Martínez believed that by 1940, when Orozco came to New York to paint the *Dive Bomber and Tank*, the relationship was over under pressure from Margarita. Recall that Orozco was involved during the last years of his life with the choreographer and dancer Nellie Campobello. Jorge Martínez, telephone interview with author, 9 July 1996.

3. Orozco, *Cartas a Margarita*, 312. Letter to Margarita Valladares, 7 October 1945.

4. José Clemente Orozco, letter to Margarita Valladares, 17 October 1945.

5. Orozco, *Cartas a Margarita*, 314, 315. Letter to Margarita Valladares, 21 October 1945.

6. Ibid., 322. Letter to Margarita Valladares, 11 November 1945.

7. Ibid., 316. Letter to Margarita Valladares, 23 October 1945.

8. Ibid., 322. Letter to Margarita Valladares, 11 November 1945.

9. Lucrecia Orozco de Herrero, interview with author, 27 June 1995, Guadalajara, Jalisco, Mexico.

10. Rufino Tamayo clipping file, Visual Art Archives, Organization of American States, Washington, D.C. Starting in the mid-1940s and into the late 1950s, Knoedler showcased Tamayo's work in one-person exhibitions every other year or so.

11. Orozco, *Cartas a Margarita*, 325. Letter to Margarita Valladares, 11 November 1946.

12. José Clemente Orozco, letter to Margarita Valladares, 16 November 1945.

13. "On the Town," *The New Yorker*, 30 November 1945, 16.

14. Ibid., 16–17.

15. Orozco, *Cartas a Margarita*, 332–33. Letters to Margarita Valladares, 9 and 12 December 1945.

16. Ibid., 330–41. Letters from 3 December 1945, through 3 January 1946.

17. Margarita Valladares de Orozco, letter to author, 3 September 1992. The exhibition at Knoedler never took place. No record of it exists in the gallery archives, nor are there any notices in the art periodicals.

18. Gómez Sicre, typed manuscript of Orozco interview, 13 February 1946, 1–3.

19. Lucrecia Orozco de Herrero, interview with author, 27 June 1995, Guadalajara, Jalisco, Mexico.

20. "Mexico on the Moon," *Time*, 30 June 1947, 8.

21. "Jose Orozco, Mural Painter, Dies in Mexico," *New York Herald Tribune*, 8 September 1949.

22. "Obituaries," *Art News* (October 1949), 66.

BIBLIOGRAPHY

Books

Albro, Ward S. *Always a Rebel: Ricardo Flores Magón and the Mexican Revolution.* Austin: University of Texas Press, 1992.

Avrich, Paul. *Kronstadt, 1921.* Princeton, N.J.: Princeton University Press, 1970.

Azuela, Mariano. *The Underdogs.* Translated by Enrique Munguía. New York: Brentano's, 1929.

Baigell, Matthew. *Dictionary of American Art.* New York: Harper & Row, 1982.

Baigell, Matthew, and Julia Williams. *Artists against War and Fascism. Papers of the First American Artists Congress.* New Brunswick, N.J.: Rutgers University Press, 1986.

Barr, Alfred H., Jr. *Defining Modern Art: Selected Writings of Alfred H. Barr, Jr.* New York: Harry N. Abrams, 1986.

————. *What Is Modern Painting?.* New York: Museum of Modern Art, 1946.

Benton, Thomas Hart. *An American in Art.* Lawrence: University Press of Kansas, 1969.

Boime, Albert. *The Academy and French Painting in the Nineteenth Century.* New Haven, Conn.: Yale University Press, 1971.

Cardoza y Aragón, Luis. *Orozco.* 1959. 3rd ed. México: Fondo de Cultura Económica, 1983.

Charlot, Jean. *The Mexican Mural Renaissance, 1920–25.* New Haven, Conn.: Yale University Press, 1962.

Christ-Janer, Albert. *Boardman Robinson.* Chicago: University of Chicago Press, 1946.

Craven, David. *Diego Rivera as Epic Modernist.* New York: G. K. Hall, 1997.

Delpart, Helen. *The Enormous Vogue of Things Mexican.* Tuscaloosa: University of Alabama Press, 1992.

Douglas, Ann. *Terrible Honesty: Mongrel Manhattan in the 1920s*. New York: Farrar, Strauss and Giroux, 1995.

Fernández, Justino. *Orozco forma e idea*. 1942. 2nd ed. México: Editorial Porrúa, S.A., 1975.

————. *Textos de Orozco*. México: Instituto de Investigaciones Estéticas, Universidad Nacional Autónoma de México, 1983.

Frampton, Kenneth. *Modern Architecture: A Critical History*. New York: Oxford University Press, 1980.

Galbraith, John Kenneth. *The Great Crash, 1929*. Boston: Houghton-Mifflin, 1955.

García Lorca, Federico. *Poet in New York*. Translated by Greg Simon and Steven F. White. New York: Noonday Press, 1988.

Goldfarb Marquis, Alice. *Alfred H. Barr, Jr.: Missionary for the Modern*. Chicago: Contemporary Books, 1989.

Goldman, Shifra M. *Contemporary Mexican Painting in a Time of Change*. Austin: University of Texas Press, 1981.

González Mello, Renato. *Orozco ¿Pintor revolucionario?* México, D.F.: Universidad Nacional Autónoma de México. Instituto de Investigaciones Estéticas, 1995.

Greene, C. *Cubism and Its Enemies*. New Haven, Conn.: Yale University Press, 1987.

Greene, Graham. *The Lawless Roads*. 27th ed. New York: Penguin Books, 1994.

————. *The Power and the Glory*. 31st ed. New York: Penguin Books, 1994.

Hambidge, Jay. *The Elements of Dynamic Symmetry*. New York: Dover, 1967.

Hart, John M. *Anarchism and the Mexican Working Class, 1860–1931*. Austin: University of Texas Press, 1987.

Helm, MacKinley. *Man of Fire: J. C. Orozco*. New York: Harcourt, Brace, 1953.

Herner de Larrea, Irene. *Diego Rivera: Paradise Lost at Rockefeller Center*. México D.F.: Edicupes, S.A. De C.V., 1987.

Hurlburt, Laurance P. *The Mexican Muralists in the United States*. Albuquerque: University of New Mexico Press, 1989.

Joachimides, Christos M., Norman Rosenthal, and Wieland Schmied. *German Art in the 20th Century. Painting and Sculpture 1900–85*. Munich: Prestel-Verlag, 1985.

Krauze, Enrique. *Francisco Villa: Entre el ángel y el fierro*. México: Fondo de Cultura Económica, 1987.

Krohn, Claus Dieter. *Wissenschaft in exil*. Munich: Campus-Verlag, 1987.

Leal, Luis. *Mariano Azuela*. México: Fondo de Cultura Económica, 1971.

Martínez, José Luis. *Zapata: Iconografía*. México: Fondo de Cultura Económica, 1982.

Martínez, Juan A. *Cuban Art and National Identity: The Vanguardia Painters, 1927–1950*. Gainesville: University Press of Florida, 1994.

May, Antoinette. *Passionate Pilgrim: The Extraordinary Life of Alma Reed*. New York: Marlowe, 1994.

Meyer, Jean. *La Cristiada, vol. 1: La guerra de los cristeros*. México, D.F.: Siglo XXI, 1973–74.

———. *Historia de los cristianos en América Latina*. Siglos XIX y XX. 2nd ed. México, D.F.: Editorial Vuelta, S.A. De C.V., 1991.

Miller, Donald L. *Lewis Mumford: A Life*. Pittsburgh: University of Pittsburgh Press, 1989.

Moyssén, Xavier, ed. *Orozco: Una relectura*. México, D.F.: Universidad Nacional Autónoma de México, 1983.

Mumford, Lewis. *Technics and Civilization*. 3rd ed. New York: Harcourt Brace, 1963.

Orozco, José Clemente. *El artista en Nueva York (cartas a Jean Charlot y textos inéditos, 1925–29)*. México, D.F.: Siglo XXI, 1971.

———. *Autobiografía*. 3rd ed. México, D.F.: Ediciones Era, S.A., 1984.

———. *Cartas a Margarita*. México, D.F.: Ediciones Era, S.A., 1987.

Orozco Valladares, Clemente. *Orozco, verdad cronológica*. Guadalajara: 1983. N.p.

Parrish, Michael E. *Anxious Decades: America in Prosperity and Depression, 1920–1941*. New York: W. W. Norton, 1992.

Paoli Bolio, Francisco J., and Enrique Montalvo. *El socialismo olvidado de Yucatán*. México: Fondo de Cultura Económica, 1977.

Paz, Octavio. *Essays on Mexican Art*. Translated by Helen Lane. New York: Harcourt Brace, 1993.

Reed, Alma. *José Clemente Orozco*. New York: Delphic Studios, 1932.

———. *Orozco*. New York: Oxford University Press, 1956.

Reyes Palma, Francisco. *FRENTE a FRENTE 1934–1938 Edición facsimilar*. México, D.F.: Centro de Estudios del Movimiento Obrero y Socialista, A.C., 1994.

Riera, José, ed. *Antología anarquista*. México: Ediciones El Caballito, 1980.

Scott, William B. *New School: A History of the New School for Social Research*. New York: Harcourt Brace, 1986.

Siqueiros, David Alfaro. *Me llamaban el Coronelazo*. 3rd ed. México, D.F.: Editorial Grijalbo, S.A., 1987.

Tibol, Raquel. *Orozco: Una vida para el arte*. México: Secretaría de Educación Pública, 1983.

Todd, Ellen Wiley. *The "New Woman" Revised: Painting and Gender Politics on Fourteenth Street*. Berkeley: University of California Press, 1993.

Vasconcelos, José. *La Flama: Los de arriba en la revolución*. México, D.F.: Compañia Editorial Continental, S.A., 1959.
———. *Obras completas*. Vol. 1. México: Fondo de Cultura Económica, 1982–83.

Articles, Chapters, Catalogs, and Announcements

American Federation of Arts. *In the Spirit of Resistance*. New York: American Federation of Arts, 1996.

The Art Center. "Mexican Art." January 19–February 14, 1928. Exhibition announcement. Orozco Papers, Visual Arts Archives, Organization of American States, Washington, D.C.

———. "Miss Barnsdall Buys Orozco's Latest Work." May 1, 1933, 7.

Art Digest. "Recent Art Books," January 7, 1933, 8.

Art News. "Diego Rivera Exhibition," October 1916, 3.

———. "Obituaries," October 1949, 66.

Brening, Margaret. "Orozco at the Downtown Gallery." *New York Post*, March 31, 1929, Sec. 1.

Brenner, Anita. "A Mexican Rebel." *The Arts* 12:4 (October 1927): 201–9.

Bueno, Miguel. "El arte de Diego Rivera atacado por el genial artista C. Orozco." *El Imparcial*, November 22, 1926, 7.

Castleman, Riva. *Art of the Forties*. New York: Museum of Modern Art and Harry N. Abrams, 1991.

Catlin, Stanton L. "Mural Census." In Detroit Institute of Art.

Chicago Arts Club. "Drawings and Paintings by José C. Orozco." June 15–29, 1928. Exhibition announcement. Orozco Papers, Visual Arts Archives, Organization of American States, Washington, D.C.

Detroit Institute of Art. *Diego Rivera: A Retrospective*. New York: W. W. Norton, 1986.

Downtown Gallery. "José Orozco: Paintings of New York City." March 26–April 15, 1929. Exhibition announcement. Orozco Papers, Visual Arts Archives, Organization of American States, Washington, D.C.

Frenzel, Ivo. "Prophet, Pioneer, Seducer: Friedrich Nietzsche's Influence on Art, Literature and Philosophy in Germany." In Joachimides, Rosenthal, and Schmied.

Galleries of Marie Sterner. "Mexico in Revolution." October 10–22, 1928. Exhibition announcement. Orozco Papers, Visual Arts Archives, Organization of American States, Washington, D.C.

Goodrich, Lloyd. "In the Galleries." *The Arts* 16:6 (February 1930): 423.

———. "The Murals of the New School." *The Arts* 17:6 (March 1931): 399–444.

Hopkins, J. H. *Orozco: A Catalogue of His Graphic Work.* Flagstaff: University of Northern Arizona Press, 1967.

Hutton, John. "'If I am to die tomorrow'—. . ." Roots and Meanings of Orozco's Zapata Entering a Peasant's Hut." *Art Institute of Chicago Museum Studies* 2:1 (Fall 1984): 38–51. Jakira, A. "As if to Slaughter." *Labor Defender* nos. 5, 6 (June 1930): 126.

Jewell, Edward Alden. "Review." *New York Times*, January 25, 1931, Sec. 5.

Johnson, Alvin. "Notes on the New School Murals." New York: The New School for Social Research, 1943.

Luther Cary, Elizabeth. "Reviews." *New York Times*, March 31, 1929, Sec. 5.

Marrozzini, Luigi, and Clemente Orozco V. *Catálogo completo de la obra grafica de Orozco.* San Juan: Instituto de Cultura Puertorriqueña, Universidad de Puerto Rico, 1970. "Mexico On the Moon." *Time*, June 30, 1947, 8.

Museum of Modern Art. *Diego Rivera.* New York: W. W. Norton, 1931.

———. *Orozco "Explains."* New York: Museum of Modern Art, 1940.

———. *20 Centuries of Mexican Art.* New York: Museum of Modern Art, 1940.

"On the Town." *The New Yorker*, November 30, 1945, 16.

Orozco, José Clemente. "New World, New Races and New Art." *Creative Art* 4:1 (January 1929): 44–46.

Oxford University Museum of Modern Art. *Orozco!* Oxford: Oxford University Museum of Modern Art, 1980.

Park, Marlene. "Lynching and Antilynching: Art and Politics in the 1930s." In *Prospects*. Vol. 18. Cambridge, Mass.: Cambridge University Press, 1993, 311–65.

Phillips, Sandra S. "The Art Criticism of Walter Pach." *Art Bulletin* 65:1 (March 1983): 106–22.

Porter, Fairfield. "Murals for Workers." *Arise* 1:4 (1935).

Ramírez, Fausto. "Artistas e inciados en la obra mural de Orozco." In Moyssén.

Reade, Helen Appelton. "Review." *Brooklyn Eagle,* February 1, 1931.

Schmeckebier, Laurance. "Orozco's Graphic Art." *Print Collector's Quarterly* (London) 21:2 (April 1934): 185–93.

Selz, Peter. *New Images of Man.* New York: Museum of Modern Art, 1959.

Sikelianos, Angelos. *Plan général du mouvement delphique.* Paris: Les Belles Lettres, 1929.

Sotheby's. "Important Latin American Paintings, Drawings and Sculpture." May 28–29, 1985. Auction catalog.

Stavitsky, Gail. *Reordering Reality: Precisionism in America.* New York: Montclair Art Museum and Harry N. Abrams, 1994.

Unpublished Materials

Brenner, Anita. Letter to Jean Charlot, January 16, 1947. Jean Charlot Papers, Thomas Hale Hamilton Library, University of Hawaii, Honolulu.

Catlin, Stanton L. Typed manuscript of Lewis Rubinstein interview, February 4, 1993. Stanton L. Catlin Papers, Syracuse, New York.

Galleries of Marie Sterner. Sales records, Sterner Papers, Archives of American Art, Washington, D.C.

García Lorca, Federico. Letter to Luis Cardoza y Aragón, April 6, 1930. Fundación Lya Kosta y Luis Cardoza y Aragón, México, D.F.

Gómez Sicre, José. Typed manuscript of José Clemente Orozco interview, February 13, 1946. José Gómez Sicre Papers, Miami, Florida.

Orozco, José Clemente. Correspondence to Margarita Valladares, 1927–34, 1940, 1945. Collection of Alfredo Orozco Valladares, Cuautla, Morelos, México.

———. Notebooks, 1931–34. Collection of Alfredo Orozco Valladares, Cuautla, Morelos, México.

Orozco de Herrero, Lucrecia. Typed response to questionnaire by author, September 5, 1995.

Reed, Alma. Letter to José Clemente Orozco, September 26, 1928. Collection of Lucrecia Orozco de Herrero, Guadalajara, Jalisco, México.

Rivas Mercado, Antonieta. Letter to Manuel Rodríguez Lozano, October 20, 1929. Manuel Rodríguez Lozano Papers, Archivos del Instituto Nacional de Bellas Artes, México, D.F.

DATE DUE